pressure cooking

for everyone

CHRONICLE BOOKS

SAN FRANCISCO

Library of Congress Cataloging-in-Publication
Data available.

ISBN 0-8118-3995-8

This edition produced exclusively for Fagor America, Inc.,
in 2002 by Chronicle Books, LLC.

Printed in Hong Kong.

Recipe developers: Rick Rodgers and Arlene Ward
Photographer: Kathryn Russell
Prop stylist: Kathy Longinaker
Food stylist: Dierdra B. Bugli
Assistant food stylist: Barbara Bugli
Design: Elizabeth Van Itallie

10 9 8 7 6 5 4 3 2 1

Chronicle Books LLC
85 Second Street
San Francisco, California 94105

www.chroniclebooks.com

table of contents

beans

risotto and grains

quick pasta sauces

vegetables

desserts and fruits

letting off **steam**: pressure cooker basics

Thank you for purchasing a Fagor Pressure Cooker. We appreciate the confidence you have placed in our company by selecting one of our many pressure cookers, and we are confident that it will give you many years of excellent service.

Fagor has been making pressure cookers for more than 45 years. All models feature a triple safety system plus a locking handle that prevents opening under pressure, so the cooking experience is completely secure. In addition, all of our models are beautifully designed with an exterior polish mirror finish, are constructed of 18/10 stainless steel with an aluminum encapsulated bottom for even heat distribution, work on all types of stovetops (gas, electric, ceramic, or induction), are U.L. (Underwriters Laboratories) approved, and come with a 10-year consumer warranty.

What are the benefits of pressure cooking?

FAST. Saves up to 70% in cooking time!

EASY. Just load the ingredients and liquids into the cooker, close the lid, bring to pressure and cook, then release and open the lid. It's that simple!

HEALTHY. Because foods are cooked under pressure, up to 50% more vitamins and minerals are retained. Also, shorter cooking times retain more nutrients in food.

SAFE. Fagor Pressure Cookers have a triple safety system that permits any possible excess pressure to escape, so the cooking experience is completely secure.

VERSATILE. All types of food can be cooked in a pressure cooker—vegetables, rice, stews, soups, chicken, fish, meats, even desserts.

ENERGY EFFICIENT. Pressure cooking conserves energy by reducing cooking times.

GREAT TASTE. The steam created inside the cooker breaks down the fibers in food in a very short time, leaving food moist and succulent, with an intense inter-mingling of flavors.

How does my pressure cooker work?

At sea level (where atmospheric pressure is 14.7 pounds per square inch [psi]), water boils at 212°F. With a pressure cooker, when the lid is properly locked into place on the cooker, an airtight seal is created trapping the steam from the boiling liquid inside. As the pressure from the steam rises, the temperature rises above the standard boiling temperature. If allowed to build to high pressure, the temperature will reach 250°F, or 38°F above the standard boiling temperature, and the pressure in the pot will be 15 pounds psi above the atmospheric pressure outside the pot. At low pressure it is 220°F and plus 5 pounds psi. *Most of the recipes in this book are cooked at high pressure.* Depending on the type of Fagor Pressure Cooker model you have purchased, you can select between 1-2 pressure settings (high and low). All Fagor Pressure Cookers are equipped with a spring-valve pressure mechanism, which is one of the many safety devices Fagor has implemented to release some steam to maintain a safe level of pressure. As pressure builds in the pressure cooker, this spring-loaded valve located in the lid compresses and raises a visual pressure indicator into an upright position, letting you know that the unit is working properly. If the pressure indicator does not appear to rise after several minutes over

high heat, you may need to check that the lid is secure and locked properly, and that the rubber gasket is in place. Remember the steam and pressure must be released before the lid can be opened.

What are some tips before I begin pressure cooking?

To ensure that everything is in working order, it's important to check all the parts of your Fagor Pressure Cooker every time you use it. Here's what to check:

1. Make sure the pressure cooker is washed well after each use. There should be no food or residue on the pot or lid. Make sure the inner part of the lid rim, the outer rim on the pot, and the rubber gasket are clean. This will reduce the risk of the lid sticking when you open the pressure cooker after cooking.

2. Remove the rubber gasket to make sure that the rubber is still flexible and is not dried out. Check for any tears or cracks. If the rubber gasket shows any sign of being dry or damaged, do not

use the pressure cooker. Replace the old part immediately with a new gasket, readily obtainable by telephoning Fagor America at 1-800-207-0806 or by obtaining an order form on our Web site, www.fagoramerica.com.

3. Check the safety valves. Since your pressure cooker has a spring-regulated valve, press or pull gently on the valve to make sure that it moves without any resistance. Each design varies; check your Fagor user's manual for the exact requirements for keeping the safety valves in working order.

How do I load my pressure cooker?

Because a pressure cooker needs space for steam to be created and room for the pressure to build, never fill your cooker more than two-thirds full. Never pack solid foods into the cooker, as it would defeat the purpose of fast cooking.

When preparing meat and poultry for cooking under pressure, brown them, without the lid on, directly in the pressure cooker. By doing so, you will be adding flavor to the dish as well as adding extra color by browning the meat or poultry first. Always brown with the lid off and usually over high or medium-high heat, in order to sear the food's surface. Marinated foods should be well drained. All meat and poultry should be patted

before browning. When browning, be careful that the burner is not too high or you will burn the oil and scorch the pot. Do not deep fry in a pressure cooker, regardless of whether the lid is on.

When steaming foods, lightly coat the surface of the steamer basket you are using. Foods, like fish, have a tendency to stick to the basket's surface. When done steaming, remove the food from the steamer basket immediately.

Positioning and locking the lid in place: Once all the ingredients are in the cooker, you can begin cooking. To open the lid, slide the safety lock to the open position. Turn the lid counterclockwise until the raised indentation on the lid is lined up with the base handle.

Building and adjusting pressure: To build pressure in a pressure cooker, the liquid inside the pot must be brought to a boil with the lid locked in place. When the liquid boils, steam is produced, pressure is created, and thus foods are cooked. Once the lid is securely locked into place, raise the burner to high heat.* As the pressure builds, you will notice the pressure indicator rise and steam will begin to escape.

Once pressure has been reached, lower the burner and begin your cooking time. Do not lower the burner heat too much, otherwise the internal

family favorites

Here are some recipes in the book that we turn to again and again for everyday meals. We've found that kids like many of these dishes, too.

Quick Chicken Soup

Minestrone

Green Pea Soup with Ham

Turkey and Root Vegetable Soup

Abilene Beef and Bean Chili

Old-Fashioned Beef Stew with Carrots and Potatoes

Yankee Pot Roast

Corned Beef Boiled Dinner

Sweet-and-Spicy BBQ Country Ribs

BBQ Chicken

Mexican Chicken in Soft Tacos

New Orleans Red Beans and Rice

Spanish Rice with Sausage

Summer Tomato and Basil Sauce

Three-Meat Bolognese Sauce

Spaghetti and Meatballs

Steamed Potatoes with Dill Butter

Quick Garlic Mashed Potatoes

Creamy Rice Pudding

Chocolate Pots de Crème

"No-Cook" Orchard Applesauce

temperature of the pressure will drop, and the steam and pressure will decrease, after which the unit will be unable to maintain the desired level of cooking pressure.

Note to electric stove users:

Since the coils on an electric stove retain heat for a long time, food often becomes overcooked when the burner is turned down for simmering (when cooking time is started). To compensate for that, two electric burners should be turned on—one on high heat, to bring the cooker to pressure, and the other for simmering, so the cooker can be moved over and the cooking time started.

How do I time my recipes?

The amount of time you cook foods is important to achieving the best results, therefore we recommend you have a kitchen timer on hand. Once the desired level of cooking pressure has been reached, set your timer, lower your burner, and begin cooking.

Because overcooked food cannot be corrected, it is better to cook unfamiliar foods for a shorter period of time than you think is necessary. You can always go back and cook foods a little longer. You will also note that some recipes have various ingredients that are added during different pressure cooking stages. We recommend that you first add the ingredients that require more time to cook, release the pressure in the cooker, add the remaining ingredients, bring to pressure again, and finish your cooking time by lowering your burner.

What about cooking at high altitudes?

If you are cooking at a high altitude, the cooking times must be longer, as water and cooking liquids come to a boil more slowly. A rule of thumb is to increase the cooking time by 5% for every 1,000 feet above the first 2,000 feet above sea level—for example, 3,000 feet above sea level, add 5% to cooking time; 4,000 feet, add 10%; and so on.

Since the cooking times increase at altitudes higher than 2,000 feet, you will also have to add more cooking liquid to compensate. There are no fixed rules, so try increasing the cooking liquid by approximately half the percentage of the additional cooking time. For example, if the cooking time is increased by 10%, increase cooking liquid by 5%.

How do I release pressure?

When the food has finished cooking, remove the pressure cooker from the burner. Although you are no longer cooking, the heat inside the cooker is very hot and foods will continue to cook until the temperature is lowered and the pressure is released.

Most of the recipes in this book call for the quick-release method, which depressurizes the cooker by turning the valve to the release position. This allows for an instant release of pressure.

Opening the pressure cooker: On all Fagor Pressure Cooker models, the pressure cooker can only be opened after all the built-up pressure has been released. As a safety feature, U.L. (Underwriters Laboratories) now requires that all units have a safety lock that prevents the cooker from being opened until there is no more pressure.

Since the food in the pressure cooker is extremely hot, use caution in opening and removing the lid. Hold the grip-like handle on the pot with one hand and turn the lid counterclockwise by grasping and turning the lid hard. Even though there is no further pressure in the pressure cooker, there will be some steam rising out. Therefore, to avoid being burned, never hold your face over the pressure cooker as you remove the lid.

How should I wash and store the pressure cooker?

As the Fagor Pressure Cooker is constructed of 18/10 stainless steel with a beautiful mirror finish on the exterior, it should be cleaned and maintained like any other piece of quality cookware.

company fare

When company's coming, the pressure cooker can help you get an elegant meal on the table in record time without any compromises in flavor or quality. The following are dishes that we have served to company with great success.

Borscht with Beef Shanks and Fresh Beets
Provençal Onion Soup
Deviled Short Ribs
Beef Brisket with Onion-Raisin Sauce
Cuban Pot Roast with Capers and Olives
Five-Spice Pork Roast
Pork Chops with Cherry–Black Currant Sauce
Rolled Butterflied Leg of Lamb
Loin Lamb Chops Dijonnaise
Veal Roast with Prosciutto, Sage, and Lemon
Osso Bucco Presto
Chicken with Tarragon-Mustard Sauce
North Beach Cioppino
Normandy Fish Chowder with Saffron
Tuna Steaks in Basque Sweet Pepper Ragout
Pinto Bean Salad with Chile Vinaigrette
Risotto with Porcini and Parmesan
Risotto with Butternut Squash and Sausage
Shrimp and Saffron Risotto
Pasta with Wild Mushroom Sauce
Artichokes with Minted Vegetable Broth
Potato Salad with Mustard and Herbs
Orange-Glazed Yams
Orange and Chocolate Marble Cheesecake
Café con Leche Flan
Ginger Crème Brûlée
Riesling Pears with Mascarpone and Almonds

After each use, wash the inside and outside of the pot and lid with mild dishwashing soap and a non-abrasive sponge, then rinse well. Never immerse the lid in water, since it may affect and damage the safety valves. Never wash the lid or rubber gasket in the dishwasher as this could damage the parts and dry out the gasket. When washing the lid, always remove the rubber gasket. Wash the rubber gasket with water and mild dishwashing soap.

After washing, towel dry all of the parts of the pressure cooker. Reposition the cleaned and dried rubber gasket seal into the lid, under the rim. IMPORTANT: When storing the pressure cooker, never lock the lid in place, since you can damage the rubber gasket, or worse yet, not be able to reopen the pressure cooker—moisture that may develop can create an almost permanent seal. Always store the lid upside down on top of the pot.

Help is but a phone call away:

If you should have questions, please telephone the Fagor Customer Service Department at 1-800-207-0806 or e-mail us your question at info@fagoramerica.com.

Web site: www.fagoramerica.com

soups
and stocks

The pressure cooker is *the* ideal tool for making quick soups and stocks. It will make more than what you'll usually need for one meal, but that's a bonus. Our freezers are filled with soups and stocks in 1-pint and 1-quart containers. It's a real joy to realize that all you have to do is defrost and heat up some homemade soup and you can have a meal on the table in no time.

Soups are more than warming winter meals. Sure, they're great served piping hot when the weather is cold, but many soups are equally tasty chilled. Instead of having the stove on for hours when the sun is blazing, use the pressure cooker to create light soups in minutes. Borscht (page 19), Minestrone (page 22), and creamy Green Pea Soup with Fresh Herbs (page 27) are three classic soups

served either hot or cold. However, when chilled these soups may be better without meat and prepared with Homemade Vegetable Stock (page 16). In cold soups, the chilled fat in the meat tends to give the soup a greasy mouth-feel no matter how well it is skimmed.

A good stock is the backbone to many dishes. Canned broth is fine, but homemade stock improves any dish and is very easy to make in the pressure cooker. Low-sodium canned brands taste best and won't add excessive salt to the finished dish. Do not use bouillon cubes. They just don't taste good, and they are much too salty to use reliably in a pressure cooker, which tends to intensify the salt flavor in foods.

tips for **soups** and **stocks**

➤ At first, pressure-cooked stocks will look cloudy, because the stock has boiled in the cooker and the fat and gelatin from the bones are suspended in the liquid. You can use the stock immediately, but it improves if refrigerated before using. Allow the strained stock to cool to room temperature, then refrigerate overnight. The fat will chill and will rise to the top of the stock, where it can be scraped off with a large spoon.

➤ Stock is made from bones and used as an ingredient in a recipe. Broth is made from meat and bones, and is seasoned to be enjoyed on its own. The two are interchangeable.

➤ Never salt stock. Often the cooking liquid in a recipe is boiled down to intensify the flavors. However, the salt will remain the same regardless of the amount of liquid.

➤ The recipes in this chapter yield good-sized amounts. Plan on freezing the leftovers! Freezer-safe plastic delicatessen containers can be found at restaurant supply stores and wholesale clubs. (Or just ask your delicatessen or supermarket if they will sell you a few.) Unfortunately, not all these containers are microwave-safe. To be on the safe side, only partially defrost the soup or stock in the container. Transfer it to a microwave-safe bowl, cover, and continue defrosting.

➤ To freeze soup or stock, skim any fat from the surface. Cool to room temperature. Pour into freezer-safe containers, leaving 1 inch of head space to allow for expansion. Freeze for up to 6 months.

➤ Most of our recipes are cooked in a liquid. The fat from the meat is transferred to the liquid and should be removed. Let the cooking liquid stand off the heat for a few minutes to allow the fat to rise to the top, and use a large spoon to skim it off.

➤ Traditionally cooked stocks are always prepared with cold water. With a pressure cooker, you can use warm or hot water with no adverse effect. The warmer water brings the cooker up to pressure more quickly, and reduces the total cooking time.

homemade **chicken stock**

This is the all-purpose stock that Arlene uses for her cooking classes. Many a particular chef has complimented her on its flavor. Chicken backs, with their high proportion of bones and a modest amount of skin, make the best stock. While they are available at most supermarkets, they can be collected from cut-up chickens (see page 58) and frozen until you have enough for a batch of stock. Save and freeze the neck and giblets — except the liver — and wings, if desired, for stock, too. Chicken wings are a second choice, as the fat in the skin will make the stock cloudy at first—it definitely needs to stand for a few hours to allow the fat to rise to the top, where it can be skimmed off.

> 2 **pounds chicken backs, all visible fat and excess skin removed**
> 1 **tablespoon vegetable oil**
> 1 **small onion, halved**
> 1 **small carrot, coarsely chopped**
> 1 **small celery rib with leaves, coarsely chopped**
> ¼ **teaspoon dried thyme**
> ¼ **teaspoon black peppercorns**
> 4 **parsley sprigs**
> 1 **bay leaf**
> 2 **quarts water**

1. Using a heavy cleaver, chop the chicken backs into 2- to 3-inch pieces. (You may ask the butcher to do this.)

2. In a 5- to 7-quart pressure cooker, heat the oil over medium-high heat. In batches, add the chicken and cook, turning occasionally, until lightly browned, about 5 minutes. Transfer to a plate and set aside.

3. Pour all but 1 tablespoon of the fat from the pot. Add the onion, carrot, and celery. Cook, stirring occasionally, until the vegetables soften, about 2 minutes. Return the chicken to the pot. Stir in the thyme, peppercorns, parsley, and bay leaf. Add the water.

4. Lock the lid in place. Bring to high pressure over high heat. Adjust the heat to maintain the pressure. Cook for 40 minutes.

5. Remove from the heat and release the pressure naturally. This will take about 20 minutes. (You can also quick-release the steam, but the natural-release cooks the stock a bit more to extract additional flavor.) Open the lid, tilting it away from you to block any escaping steam. Strain the stock into a large bowl. Cool completely. Cover and refrigerate overnight.

6. Using a large spoon, remove the chilled fat from the surface of the stock. (The stock can be prepared up to 3 days ahead, stored in an airtight container and refrigerated, or frozen for up to 6 months.)

Makes about 2 quarts
40 minutes at high pressure

homemade **beef stock**

While we have been known to use a can of chicken broth, canned beef broth isn't as reliable. Before we became pressure-cooker fans, making homemade beef stock was admittedly a chore rather than a pleasure. Now, whenever we see beef bones at a good price at the market, it's a cinch to whip up a batch. Plainly put, the flavor of homemade stock is incomparable to canned stock, and it is especially important in recipes where the flavor of the stock isn't masked by other ingredients, such as Provençal Onion Soup (page 25).

1 tablespoon vegetable oil
2 pounds beef bones, sawed by the butcher into
    1- to 2-inch-thick pieces
1 pound cross-cut meaty beef shanks
1 small onion, coarsely chopped
1 small carrot, coarsely chopped
1 small celery rib with leaves, coarsely chopped
1 garlic clove, crushed
1 tablespoon tomato paste
¼ teaspoon dried thyme
¼ teaspoon whole black peppercorns
4 sprigs fresh parsley
1 bay leaf
2 quarts water

1. In a 5- to 7-quart pressure cooker, heat the oil over medium-high heat. In batches, add bones and shanks and cook, turning occasionally, until lightly browned, about 6 minutes. Transfer to a plate and set aside.

2. Pour all but 1 tablespoon of the fat from the pot. Add the onion, carrot, celery, and garlic. Cook, stirring occasionally, until the vegetables begin to soften, about 2 minutes. Return the bones and shanks to the pot. Stir in the tomato paste, thyme, peppercorns, parsley, and bay leaf. Add the water. Lock the lid in place and bring to high pressure over high heat. Adjust the heat to maintain the pressure. Cook for 1 hour.

3. Remove from the heat and release the steam naturally. This will take about 20 minutes. (You can also quick-release the steam, but the natural-release cooks the stock a bit more to extract additional flavor.) Open the lid, tilting it away from you to block any escaping steam. Strain the stock into a large bowl. Cool completely. Cover and refrigerate overnight.

4. Using a large spoon, remove the chilled fat from the surface of the stock. (The stock can be prepared up to 3 days ahead, stored in an airtight container and refrigerated, or frozen for up to 6 months.)

Veal Stock: Substitute veal shanks and bones for the beef.

Makes about 2 quarts
1 hour at high pressure

homemade **fish stock**

Fish stock is one of the quickest stocks to make because the fish bones are thinner than their meat and poultry counterparts. Even so, the pressure cooker efficiently extracts the flavor from the bones in record time. As fish bones tend to foam during cooking, skim off any foam that forms while the stock comes to a boil, drizzle a little oil on top before closing the lid, and use a natural-release method to cut down on sputtering. Fish stock is delicate; if freezing, use within 2 months.

2½ pounds assorted bones, heads (no gills), and trimmings from white-fleshed fish (avoid oily varieties like salmon, bluefish, or whiting), chopped into large pieces
1 medium onion, coarsely chopped
2 medium celery ribs with leaves, coarsely chopped
6 parsley sprigs
½ cup dry white wine, such as Sauvignon Blanc
1½ quarts water, as needed
¼ teaspoon dried thyme
¼ teaspoon whole black peppercorns
1 bay leaf
2 teaspoons vegetable oil

1. In a 5- to 7-quart pressure cooker, combine the fish, onion, celery, and parsley. Add the wine. Pour in enough water to cover the fish completely, but the cooker should be no more than two-thirds full. Bring to a boil, uncovered, over high heat, skimming off any foam that rises to the surface. Add the thyme, peppercorns, and bay leaf. Drizzle the oil over the stock.

2. Lock the lid in place. Bring to high pressure over high heat. Adjust the heat to maintain the pressure. Cook for 10 minutes. Remove from the heat.

Allow the pressure to drop naturally. Open the lid, tilting it away from you to block any escaping steam. Strain the stock through a colander into a medium bowl. Cool completely. (The stock can be prepared up to 2 days ahead, stored in an airtight container and refrigerated, or frozen for up to 2 months.)

———

Makes about 2 quarts
10 minutes at high pressure

homemade vegetable stock

You don't have to be vegetarian to appreciate a good vegetable stock. It is another ingredient that is hard to find in an acceptable commercial version (some of them are too heavy on cabbage and beets). You'll use this stock in vegetarian dishes, of course, but try it as a substitute for meat or poultry stocks, soups, or stews. It's delicious on its own as a soup, perhaps with some pasta, rice, or beans stirred in. A good homemade vegetable stock relies on potatoes (to give the stock body) and lots of garlic (for flavor), and not on a hodge-podge of tired specimens from the vegetable cooler. Use fresh, flavorful ingredients, and don't alter the recipe so you get variable results all the time. (Would you want a beef or chicken stock that tasted different every time you made it?)

2 tablespoons oil
2 medium onions, unpeeled, cut crosswise in half
3 medium carrots, chopped
3 medium celery ribs with leaves, chopped
1 large (about 13 ounces) russet or Burbank potato, scrubbed, unpeeled, and cut into 2-inch chunks
1 head garlic, cloves crushed under a heavy knife, and peeled
2 quarts water, as needed
6 parsley sprigs
¼ teaspoon dried thyme
1 bay leaf
1 teaspoon salt
½ teaspoon whole black peppercorns

1. In a 5- to 7-quart pressure cooker, heat the oil over medium-high heat. Add the onions, carrots, celery, potato, and garlic. Cook, stirring occasionally, until the onions are golden and a light brown film forms on the bottom of the cooker, about 6 minutes.

2. Add enough water to come halfway up the sides of the cooker, about 2 quarts. Stir in the parsley, thyme, bay leaf, salt, and peppercorns.

3. Lock the lid in place. Bring to high pressure over high heat. Adjust the heat to maintain the pressure. Cook for 20 minutes. Remove from the heat and quick-release the pressure. Open the lid, tilting it away from you to block any escaping steam. Strain the stock through a colander into a medium bowl. Cool completely. (The stock can be prepared up to 3 days ahead, stored in an airtight container and refrigerated, or frozen for up to 6 months.)

Makes about 2 quarts
20 minutes at high pressure

quick chicken soup

Arlene devised this recipe when she had a bad cold and wanted some restorative chicken soup in a hurry. In a recent cooking contest for "Jewish penicillin" (what many New Yorkers call chicken soup because it is used to "cure" so many minor ailments), all of the well-seasoned contestants admitted that they used canned chicken broth or bouillon cubes to give their soup a boost. If it's good enough for a Jewish grandmother, it's good enough for us! If you are a white-meat person, use chicken breasts, but the thighs hold up better in the pressure cooker.

- 2 tablespoons vegetable oil
- 1½ pounds boneless, skinless chicken thighs
- 1 medium onion, chopped
- 2 medium carrots, cut into ½-inch-thick rounds
- 2 medium celery ribs with leaves, cut into ¼-inch-thick slices
- 4 cups water
- 2 cups canned low-sodium chicken broth
- ¼ teaspoon dried thyme
- 1 small bay leaf
- ½ teaspoon salt, plus more to taste
- ¼ teaspoon freshly ground black pepper, plus more to taste
- 1 cup fine egg noodles
- 2 tablespoons chopped fresh parsley

1. In a 5- to 7-quart pressure cooker, heat 1 tablespoon of the oil over medium heat. Add the chicken thighs and cook, turning once, until browned, about 5 minutes. Transfer the chicken to a plate and set aside.

2. Add the remaining 1 tablespoon oil to the pot and heat. Add the onion, carrots, and celery. Cook, stirring occasionally, until the vegetables are beginning to soften, about 2 minutes. Stir in the water, broth, thyme, bay leaf, ¼ teaspoon salt, and ½ teaspoon pepper, scraping up any browned bits on the bottom of the pot. Return the chicken to the pot.

3. Lock the lid in place. Bring to high pressure over high heat. Adjust the temperature to maintain the pressure. Cook for 8 minutes. Remove from the heat and quick-release the pressure. Open the lid, tilting it away from you to block any escaping steam. Transfer the chicken to a cutting board and set aside.

4. Skim any fat from the surface of the cooking liquid. Bring to a boil, uncovered, over high heat. Season the soup with additional salt and pepper. Stir in the noodles and parsley. Reduce the heat to medium and cook, uncovered, until the noodles are tender, about 9 minutes.

5. Cut the chicken into bite-sized pieces. Return to the soup and heat through. Serve hot.

Chicken Rice Soup: Substitute ½ cup long-grain rice for the noodles. Simmer until tender, about 15 minutes.

Straciatella: This makes delicately delicious strands of cheese and egg in the soup. Delete the noodles. In a small bowl, mix 2 large eggs, 2 tablespoons freshly grated Parmesan cheese, and the parsley until well combined. Stirring the simmering soup constantly, drizzle the egg mixture into the soup. Cook uncovered until the strands are set, about 1 minute.

Makes 8 to 12 servings
8 minutes at high pressure

borscht with beef shanks and fresh beets

Borscht is a rib-sticking soup that is usually considered winter fare, but doesn't need to be reserved for cold weather. During the winter, the borscht with beef shanks can be served hot with chunks of tender cooked beef. But in the summer, chilled borscht (made without the beef shanks) is wonderful as a refreshing lunch or light supper. If your beets don't have any greens, don't worry—they add a touch of color and flavor to the soup, but they are entirely optional. And be flexible with the cooking time needed for the beets, as their tenderness varies from bunch to bunch.

- 2 tablespoons vegetable oil
- 1 pound cross-cut meaty beef shanks
- 1 medium onion, chopped
- 2 medium carrots, cut into ½-inch dice
- 2 medium celery ribs, cut into ½-inch dice
- 1 garlic clove, minced
- 5 cups water
- 2 cups Homemade Beef Stock (page 14) or canned low-sodium broth
- 1 cup chopped seeded plum tomatoes or one 14½-ounce can tomatoes in juice, drained and chopped
- ½ teaspoon dried thyme
- 1 bay leaf
- ½ teaspoon salt, plus more to taste
- ¼ teaspoon freshly ground black pepper, plus more to taste
- 3 medium beets, preferably with greens attached
- 4 cups thinly sliced green cabbage (about ½ large head)
- ¼ cup red wine vinegar
- 2 tablespoons light brown sugar
- ¼ cup chopped fresh dill
- Sour cream, at room temperature, for serving

1. In a 5- to 7-quart or larger pressure cooker, heat 1 tablespoon of the oil over medium-high heat. Add the beef shanks and brown on both sides, about 4 minutes. Transfer to a plate and set aside.

2. Add the remaining 1 tablespoon oil to the pot and heat over medium heat. Add the onion, carrots, celery, and garlic and cook, stirring occasionally, just until beginning to soften, about 3 minutes. Return the beef shanks and any juices on the plate to the pot. Stir in the water, stock, tomatoes, thyme, bay leaf, ½ teaspoon salt, and ¼ teaspoon pepper. Lock the lid in place. Bring to high pressure over high heat. Adjust the heat to maintain the pressure. Cook for 30 minutes. Remove from the heat and quick-release the pressure. Open the lid, tilting it away from you to block any escaping steam. Remove the beef shanks and bay leaf. Discard the bones and cut the meat into bite-sized pieces; set aside.

3. Meanwhile, cut the greens from the beets, discarding the stems. Rinse the greens well (they can be sandy) and chop coarsely. Peel the beets and cut into ½-inch dice.

4. Add the cabbage, beets and greens, vinegar, and brown sugar to the pot. Lock the lid in place and bring to high pressure over high heat. Adjust the heat to maintain the pressure. Cook for 8 minutes. Remove from the heat and quick-release the steam. Open the lid, tilting it away from you to block any escaping steam.

5. Stir the beef and dill into the soup and cook,

uncovered, to heat through, about 2 minutes. Season to taste with salt and pepper. Serve hot in individual bowls, topping each serving with a dollop of sour cream.

Chilled Borscht: Delete the beef shanks. Cook the vegetables in 2 tablespoons vegetable oil. If desired, substitute 2 cups Homemade Vegetable Stock (page 16) or canned vegetable broth for the beef stock.

─────────

Makes 8 to 10 servings
30 minutes at high pressure for beef,
then 8 minutes at high pressure for beets

hearty lentil and pasta soup

Pasta e fagioli, literally "pasta and beans," is a thick, stand-your-spoon-up-in-the-pot dish made all over Italy. Arlene makes her version with lentils, which give a hearty bean flavor but need no presoaking. When she used to make it the traditional stove-simmered way, it took a couple of hours. Now with the pressure cooker, it takes under 10 minutes. Leftover soup will thicken upon standing; thin with additional stock or water.

2 tablespoons olive oil
4 ounces pancetta or bacon, coarsely chopped
1 large onion, chopped
4 medium celery ribs, cut into ½-inch dice
5 medium carrots, cut into ½-inch dice
3 garlic cloves, chopped
½ teaspoon dried thyme
½ teaspoon dried oregano
1 bay leaf
1 pound dried lentils, rinsed and sorted to remove stones
One 15-ounce can tomatoes in juice, drained and puréed in a blender
5 cups water
2 cups Homemade Beef Stock (page 14) or canned low-sodium broth
1 teaspoon salt, plus more to taste
¼ teaspoon freshly ground black pepper, plus more to taste
8 ounces small pasta for soup, such as ditalini (1½ cups)
Freshly grated Parmesan cheese, for serving

1. In a 5- to 7-quart pressure cooker, heat the oil over medium heat. Add the pancetta or bacon and cook, turning occasionally, until crisp, about 5 min-utes. Using a slotted spoon, transfer the meat to paper towels and set aside.

2. Pour out all but 2 tablespoons of the fat in the pot. Add the onion, celery, carrots, and garlic and cook, stirring occasionally, just until the vegetables begin to soften, about 3 minutes. Stir in the thyme, oregano, and bay leaf. Add the lentils and stir well. Stir in the tomatoes, then the water and stock. Season with 1 teaspoon salt and ¼ teaspoon pepper.

3. Lock the lid in place. Bring to high pressure over high heat. Adjust the heat to maintain pressure. Cook for 8 minutes. Remove from the heat and quick-release the pressure. Open the lid, tilting it away from you to block any escaping steam. Check the lentils for doneness; they should be barely tender. If necessary, simmer, uncovered, until tender. Season the lentils with additional salt and pepper. Stir in the pancetta.

4. Meanwhile, in a large pot of lightly salted water over high heat, cook the pasta until barely tender, about 10 minutes. Drain well.

5. To serve, spoon the pasta into bowls and top with the soup. Serve immediately, with the cheese passed on the side.

Makes 8 to 12 servings
8 minutes at high pressure

minestrone

When we make minestrone, we rarely make it the same way twice, instead improvising with the vegetables in season. For example, when fresh cranberry beans are in season in late summer, we substitute 1 cup of fresh beans for the canned ones and cook the fresh beans with the rest of the vegetables in Step 1. (Late summer is also the time to serve the soup at room temperature, just the way they do in Tuscany during hot weather.) In winter, the soup can be turned into Ribollita (recipe follows). If necessary, omit the fresh basil and add ½ teaspoon dried basil to the soup with the other dried herbs. We encourage you to use this recipe as a springboard for your own version.

> 7 cups Homemade Chicken Stock (page 13),
> canned low-sodium broth, or water
> ½ large head escarole, well rinsed and coarsely
> chopped (4 cups)
> One 28-ounce can tomatoes in juice, drained and
> coarsely chopped
> 6 ounces green beans, cut into ½-inch lengths
> 1 medium onion, chopped
> 2 medium carrots, cut into ½-inch dice
> 4 garlic cloves
> ½ teaspoon salt, plus more to taste
> ⅛ teaspoon dried oregano
> ⅛ teaspoon dried rosemary
> ¼ teaspoon freshly ground black pepper, plus
> more to taste
> 1 medium zucchini, cut into ½-inch dice
> ½ cup chopped fresh basil
> ⅓ cup small pasta for soup, such as ditalini
> 1 cup dried cannellini (white kidney) beans, soaked,
> cooked, and drained, or one 15-ounce can beans,
> drained and rinsed
> Freshly grated Parmesan cheese, for serving

1. In a 5- to 7-quart pressure cooker, combine the stock, escarole, tomatoes, green beans, onion, carrots, garlic, ½ teaspoon salt, oregano, rosemary, and ¼ teaspoon pepper. Lock the lid in place. Bring to high pressure over high heat. Adjust the heat to maintain the pressure. Cook for 10 minutes.

2. Remove from the heat and quick-release the pressure. Open the lid, tilting it away from you to block any escaping steam. Add the zucchini, basil, and pasta. Cook over medium heat, uncovered, until the pasta is tender, about 10 minutes. Add the beans and cook for 1 minute to heat through. Season with additional salt and pepper.

3. Serve hot or cooled to room temperature, with the cheese passed on the side.

Ribollita: Ribollita means "reboiled," so its very name explains that this recipes is a great way to use leftover minestrone. The exact proportions depend on the amount of soup and the size of the baking dish. Preheat the oven to 350°F. Pour half of the soup into a deep baking dish. Top with 4 to 6 slices of toasted crusty Italian bread, then a good sprinkling of freshly grated Parmesan cheese. Repeat with the remaining soup, bread, and cheese, drizzling the top with extra-virgin olive oil. Bake until the soup is simmering and the cheese is golden, 30 to 40 minutes. Serve from the dish.

Makes 8 to 12 servings
10 minutes at high pressure

turkey and root vegetable soup

Are you one of those people who loves to make turkey soup from the carcass of the holiday bird? Well, this soup provides those nostalgic flavors without having to roast a whole turkey first. Frugality is another benefit of this soup, as it uses turkey drumsticks, one of the most inexpensive items in the poultry case. If you have chicken stock or broth, use it, but water also makes a good soup.

3 medium turkey drumsticks (2 pounds total)
1 tablespoon vegetable oil
2 medium leeks, white and pale green parts only, chopped, well rinsed, and drained (1 cup)
1 large carrot, cut into ½-inch rounds
1 large parsnip, cut into ½-inch rounds
5 cups Homemade Chicken Stock (page 13), canned low-sodium broth, or water
½ teaspoon dried thyme
¼ teaspoon dried rosemary
1 bay leaf
½ teaspoon salt, plus more to taste
¼ teaspoon freshly ground black pepper, plus more to taste
2 tablespoons chopped fresh parsley

1. Using a sharp knife, pull the skin from each drumstick, cutting it off at the drumstick knob. Don't bother to remove the skin remaining around the knob.

2. In a 5- to 7-quart pressure cooker, heat the oil over medium heat. In batches, if necessary, add the drumsticks and cook, turning occasionally, until lightly browned, about 5 minutes. Transfer the drumsticks to a plate and set aside.

3. Add the leeks, carrot, and parsnip to the pot and cook, stirring occasionally, until they begin to soften, about 2 minutes. Return the drumsticks to the pot and add the stock, thyme, rosemary, bay leaf, ½ teaspoon salt, and ¼ teaspoon pepper.

4. Lock the lid in place. Bring to high pressure over high heat. Adjust the heat to maintain the pressure. Cook for 30 minutes. Remove the pot from the heat and quick-release the pressure. Open the lid, tilting it away from you to block any escaping steam.

5. Transfer the drumsticks to a cutting board and let cool until easy to handle. Remove the meat from the drumsticks, taking care to discard the long, thin sinews. Coarsely chop the meat into bite-sized pieces and discard the bones and sinews.

6. Skim off any fat on the surface of the soup. Stir in the chopped turkey and parsley. Cook, uncovered, over medium heat, until piping hot, about 3 minutes. Season with additional salt and pepper. Serve hot.

Turkey and Rice Soup: Stir ⅓ cup long-grain rice into the soup with the turkey and parsley. Simmer over medium heat until the rice is tender, about 15 minutes.

Makes 8 to 10 servings
30 minutes at high pressure

provençal onion soup

Rick learned to make this intriguingly seasoned soup at an early-career restaurant job during his college days, and he's been making it ever since. It's a bit different from the one served in Parisian bistros, with tomatoes and a hint of ground cloves flavoring the soup and a bread-and-cheese topping that is applied at the table and not broiled. The pressure cooker doesn't cut down on the time needed to cook the onions until golden and tender, but once that's out of the way, the soup will be finished in less than 10 minutes.

- 3 tablespoons unsalted butter
- 2 tablespoons olive oil
- 4 medium onions, thinly sliced into half-moons (6 cups)
- 1 garlic clove, finely chopped
- ¼ teaspoon dried thyme
- ¼ teaspoon ground cloves
- 1 bay leaf
- ½ cup dry white wine
- 6 cups Homemade Beef Stock (page 14) or canned low-sodium beef broth
- One 28-ounce can tomatoes in juice, drained and chopped
- ½ teaspoon salt, plus more to taste
- ¼ teaspoon freshly ground black pepper, plus more to taste
- Sliced, toasted French bread, for serving
- Shredded Gruyère or Swiss cheese, for serving

1. In a 5- to 7-quart pressure cooker, heat the butter and oil over medium-high heat. Add the onions and cook, uncovered, stirring occasionally, until very tender and golden, about 15 minutes. Stir in the garlic, thyme, cloves, and bay leaf and cook for 1 minute.

2. Add the wine and bring to a boil. Stir in the stock, tomatoes, ½ teaspoon salt, and ¼ teaspoon pepper. Lock the lid in place. Bring to high pressure over high heat. Adjust the heat to maintain the pressure. Cook for 6 minutes. Remove from the heat and quick-release the pressure. Open the lid, tilting it away from you to block any escaping steam.

3. Remove the bay leaf. Season the soup with additional salt and pepper. Serve the soup hot, with the bread and cheese on the side, so each person can top the soup with bread and cheese as they wish.

Makes 8 to 10 servings
6 minutes at high pressure

green pea soup with ham

Split pea soup is one of the biggest stumbling blocks for the pressure cooker, because the dried peas create a starchy foam that clogs up the cooker's valves. Arlene takes the attitude that with this deliciously easy pea soup made with frozen peas, who needs to fuss with temperamental split peas? There are lots of variations—we are especially fond of the Curried and Herb versions, which can be served chilled for a light meal on a warm summer's day. One tip: Slice the vegetables quite thin (about ⅛ inch thick or less) so they become tender in 3 minutes of pressure cooking. If they aren't tender, pressure cook again for 1 minute.

1 tablespoon vegetable oil
½ cup chopped smoked or boiled ham (see Note)
1 small onion, thinly sliced
1 small carrot, thinly sliced
1 small celery rib with leaves, thinly sliced
1 medium Idaho potato, peeled and very thinly sliced
One 10-ounce package frozen peas (no need to defrost)
2 cups Homemade Chicken Stock (page 13) or canned low-sodium broth
½ teaspoon salt, plus more to taste
⅛ teaspoon freshly ground black pepper, plus more to taste
¼ cup heavy cream

1. In a 5- to 7-quart pressure cooker, heat the oil over medium-high heat. Add the ham and cook until browned, about 5 minutes. Remove the ham with a slotted spoon, leaving any oil in the pot, and set the ham aside.

2. Add the onion, carrot, celery, and potato to the pot. Cook until the vegetables soften, about 2 minutes. Add the frozen peas, stock, ½ teaspoon salt, and ⅛ teaspoon pepper. Bring to a boil over high heat. Lock the lid in place. Bring to high pressure over high heat. Adjust the heat to maintain pressure.

3. Cook for 3 minutes. Remove from the heat and quick-release the pressure. Open the lid, tilting it away from you to block any escaping steam. Using a hand-blender, blender, or food processor, purée the soup. Stir in the cream and reserved ham and heat through. Season with additional salt and pepper. Serve hot.

Note: For more ham flavor, make a ham hock stock. Place 1 smoked ham hock, 1 small onion, 1 small carrot (both halved, not chopped), and a pinch of thyme in a pressure cooker. Add 3 cups warm water. Lock the lid in place. Bring to high pressure over high heat. Adjust the heat to maintain pressure. Cook for 20 minutes. Remove the lid. Strain the stock. Remove and discard the skin and bones, and finely chop the ham meat. Substitute the ham stock and its meat for the chicken stock and smoked or boiled ham. You will not have to brown the hock meat in oil, as it will be more flavorful than delicatessen ham.

Curried Green Pea Soup: Delete the ham. In Step 2, after the vegetables are softened, add 1¼ teaspoons curry powder and stir until it releases its aroma, about 30 seconds. Serve warm or chilled.

Green Pea Soup with Fresh Herbs: Delete the ham. Stir 1 tablespoon finely chopped fresh mint, dill, or tarragon into the soup. If desired, top each serving with a drizzle of additional heavy cream and a pinch of chopped fresh herbs. Serve warm or chilled.

Makes 4 to 6 servings
3 minutes at high pressure

zucchini and mushroom soup

This light but creamy soup with the herbaceous flavor of fresh dill will become a secret weapon in your artillery of quick-and-easy recipes. A food processor makes fast work of shredding the zucchini and chopping the mushrooms. With those chores out of the way, the pressure cooker will make the soup in minutes, one that is sophisticated enough for company yet homey enough for a satisfying weekend lunch.

2 tablespoons unsalted butter
1 large onion, chopped
12 ounces white mushrooms, chopped
2 garlic cloves, minced
6 small (1½ pounds) zucchini, trimmed and
    shredded
1 tablespoon sweet Hungarian paprika
4½ cups Homemade Chicken Stock (page 13)
    or canned low-sodium chicken broth
½ teaspoon salt, plus more to taste
¼ teaspoon freshly ground black pepper, plus
    more to taste
¼ cup all-purpose flour
1½ tablespoons chopped fresh dill
Sour cream, for serving

1. In a 5- to 7-quart pressure cooker, melt the butter over medium heat. Add the onion and cook until softened, about 2 minutes. Add the mushrooms and garlic and cook until the mushrooms begin to soften, about 2 minutes. Stir in the zucchini and paprika. Add 4 cups of the stock, and ½ teaspoon salt and ¼ teaspoon pepper.

2. Lock the lid in place. Bring to high pressure over high heat. Adjust the heat to maintain the pressure. Cook for 8 minutes. Remove from the heat and quick-release the pressure. Open the lid, tilting it away from you to block any escaping steam.

3. Place the uncovered pressure cooker over medium-low heat and bring the soup to a simmer. In a medium bowl, whisk the remaining ½ cup stock and the flour until smooth. Whisk into the soup. Simmer until the soup is thickened and no trace of raw flour flavor remains, about 5 minutes. Stir in the dill, and season with additional salt and pepper.

4. Serve hot, topping each serving with a dollop of sour cream.

Zucchini and Wild Mushroom Soup: Dried mushrooms cook quickly in a pressure cooker without soaking. Rinse ½ cup (½ ounce) dried porcini mushrooms under cold running water to remove any grit. Add the rinsed mushrooms to the soup with the fresh mushrooms.

Makes 8 to 12 servings
8 minutes at high pressure

meat main courses

Few foods are as satisfying and comforting as a meat stew. But the busier we get, the less time we have to cook those delicious stews, ragouts, pot roasts, and chilis. Other casualties of the "cook it quick" craze are tough meats that need long simmering to become tender and succulent. How can we turn our backs on such favorites as lamb and veal shanks, corned beef, beef brisket, and veal breast?

Thanks to the pressure cooker, you'll never have to scurry to find the time to cook these mouthwatering dishes again. The steam and pressure combine to tenderize tough meats in a fraction of their traditional cooking times. With a little attention to detail (and a good kitchen timer), even tender chops and roasts can be prepared in the pressure cooker.

tips for meats

➤ In general, tough cuts of meat (beef chuck, bottom round, brisket, shanks, and short ribs; lamb shanks and shoulder; veal breast, shoulder, and osso bucco; pork ribs and shoulder) work best in the pressure cooker. Leaner, more tender cuts, such as pork loin and pork and lamb chops, can be prepared in the pressure cooker if cooked at reduced times to avoid overcooking and drying out.

➤ Avoid generic meats labeled "stewing meat," because you never know what cut of meat you're getting. Even if you buy a specific cut of cubed meat, such as chuck, most butchers tend to cube them too small. Buy the specific roast and cut it into pieces about 1½-inch square. Smaller cubes can easily overcook and get mushy and stringy.

➤ When browning batches of cubed meat for a stew in the cooker, save time by browning some of the cubes in a separate skillet. If desired, pour 1 cup of the cooking liquid (broth, wine, or water) into the skillet and scrape up any browned bits with a wooden spoon; use this liquid as part of the required amount in the recipe.

➤ When seasoning meats with salt and pepper, combine the two seasonings in a small bowl; this mixture seasons the meat much more evenly than using each condiment separately.

➤ When tying large cuts of meat, leave two 12-inch lengths of string hanging from both ends. Use the strings to lift and turn the meat—you won't need a meat fork, which pierces the meat and releases juices.

➤ Most of our recipes are cooked in a liquid. The fat from the meat is transferred to the liquid and should be removed. Let the cooking liquid stand off the heat for a few minutes to allow the fat to rise to the top, and use a large spoon to skim it off.

➤ Some of the meat recipes use relatively small amounts of liquid. If necessary, increase the liquid to meet your cooker's minimum liquid requirement. Before making a gravy, pour off some of the cooking liquid. Gradually add the thickening ingredient to get the desired thickness.

➤ Pressure cooking adds steam to the food, which can dilute the flavor of the cooking liquid. This is easily remedied by boiling the skimmed cooking liquid for a few minutes to concentrate the flavors.

➤ If the recipe calls for wine, use a good, drinkable brand—never use "cooking wine," which is made from inferior wine and heavily salted. To disperse any alcohol flavors that could intensify in the cooker, add the wine to the pot right after cooking the seasoning vegetables, and allow it to come to a boil before adding the other ingredients.

➤ When thickening a sauce with dissolved cornstarch or *beurre manie* (a flour-and-butter paste), remember that the liquid must come to a boil in order to activate the thickening. Cornstarch-thickened sauces will thicken almost immediately, if added to simmering liquid. Simmer sauces thickened with *beurre manie* for about 5 minutes to remove any raw flour taste. If a sauce seems too thick, thin with broth or water. If it is too thin, add more dissolved cornstarch (even if it was originally thickened with *beurre manie*).

➤ Let roasts stand for at least 10 minutes before slicing. This allows the juices to settle and makes for easier slicing.

➤ In meat-and-bean dishes, such as chili, cook the beans separately and add them to the meat just before serving. It is difficult to guess the cooking time of dried beans, and you can easily overcook the meat while trying to get the beans tender.

rolled **butterflied** leg of **lamb**

When company is coming and you're short on time, make this extraordinary stuffed leg of lamb. Time it carefully to ensure medium-rare meat.

One 3-pound boneless leg of lamb, rolled and tied

¼ teaspoon salt, plus more to taste

¼ teaspoon freshly ground black pepper, plus more to taste

2 tablespoons drained and chopped sun-dried tomatoes in oil

2 tablespoons chopped fresh parsley

1 teaspoon chopped fresh rosemary or ½ teaspoon dried rosemary

1 garlic clove, finely chopped

1 tablespoon olive oil

¾ cup hearty red wine, such as Zinfandel

¾ cup Homemade Beef Stock (page 14) or canned low-sodium broth

2 tablespoons water

1½ tablespoons cornstarch

1 tablespoon Dijon mustard (optional)

1. Untie the roast and open it up on the work surface. Using a sharp knife, cut one or two flaps of the meat almost parallel to the work surface. Open up the flaps like a book.

2. In a small bowl, mix ¼ teaspoon salt and ¼ teaspoon pepper. Season the meat with half of the mixture. Sprinkle with the sun-dried tomatoes, parsley, rosemary, and garlic. Roll up the lamb. Using kitchen twine, tie crosswise at 2-inch intervals, then lengthwise. Season the outside of the meat with the remaining salt-and-pepper mixture.

3. In a 5- to 7-quart pressure cooker, heat the oil over medium-high heat. Add the lamb and cook, turning occasionally, until lightly browned, about 4 minutes. Transfer the lamb to a plate and set aside.

4. Add the wine and bring to a boil, stirring up the browned bits on the bottom of the pot with a wooden spoon. Stir in the broth. Return the lamb to the cooker.

5. Lock the lid in place. Bring to high pressure over high heat. Adjust the heat to maintain the pressure. Cook for 20 minutes. Remove from the heat and quick-release the pressure. Open the lid, tilting it away from you to block any escaping steam. Insert a meat thermometer in the center of the lamb. It should read 115° to 120°F. The internal temperature of the lamb will rise 5° to 10°F while standing. Transfer the lamb to a carving board and let stand for 10 minutes. Let the cooking liquid stand for 5 minutes.

6. Skim off any fat from the surface of the cooking liquid. Return the pot to medium heat and bring to a simmer. Place the water in a small bowl, sprinkle with the cornstarch, and stir to dissolve. Stir into the simmering broth and cook until thickened. Remove from the heat and whisk in the mustard. Season with additional salt and pepper.

7. Remove the strings, carve the lamb, and serve with the sauce on the side.

Makes 6 to 8 servings
20 minutes at high pressure

loin lamb chops dijonnaise

This is the recipe of Arlene's that made Rick a pressure-cooker convert. The trick is to use thick-cut lamb chops—regular, thin-cut chops will overcook. You'll have to ask your butcher to cut them specially for you—some butchers may balk at the thickness, but instruct them to do as you ask. The timing depends on the doneness of the meat. We find that 3 minutes of pressure cooking yields a perfect, medium-rare chop. One chop will be enough for delicate appetites, but you can stack up to six chops in the cooker, if you wish, as long as you don't go higher than two-thirds of the height of the pot.

Four 8-ounce loin lamb chops, cut 2 inches thick
1 tablespoon olive oil
2 garlic cloves, crushed and peeled
2 quarter-sized pieces fresh ginger, unpeeled
4 sprigs fresh rosemary or 1 teaspoon dried rosemary
1/8 teaspoon salt, plus more to taste
1/8 teaspoon freshly ground black pepper, plus more to taste
1/4 cup hearty red wine, such as Zinfandel
2 tablespoons Homemade Beef Stock (page 14), canned low-sodium broth, or water (see Note)
1 tablespoon Dijon mustard
1/2 teaspoon Japanese soy sauce

1. Trim and discard the fat from the perimeter of each chop. In a 5- to 7-quart pressure cooker, heat the oil over medium-high heat until very hot but not smoking. Add the chops and brown the underside, about 2 minutes. Turn the chops, add the garlic and ginger to the pot, and brown the other side. Transfer the chops to a plate. Place a rosemary sprig on each chop or sprinkle each with 1/4 teaspoon of the dried rosemary. Season with 1/8 teaspoon salt and 1/8 teaspoon pepper.

2. Working quickly, add the red wine to the pot, then place the rack in the pot. Place the chops on the rack. Lock the lid in place. Bring to high pressure over high heat. (If the cooker doesn't come up to pressure, add 1/4 cup water.) Cook for 3 minutes. Remove from the heat and quick-release the pressure. Open the lid, tilting it away from you to block any escaping steam. Using kitchen tongs, transfer the chops to a serving platter.

3. Discard the ginger, but keep the garlic in the pot. Add the stock, mustard, and soy sauce. Bring to a boil over high heat, crushing the garlic into the sauce. Cook just until thickened, about 30 seconds (or slightly longer if you added water to the cooker). Season with additional salt and pepper. Pour the sauce over the chops. Serve immediately.

Note: If desired, substitute 2 tablespoons store-bought veal demi-glace for the beef stock. It gives the sauce an incredible finesse.

Makes 2 to 4 servings
3 minutes at high pressure

lamb shanks with garlic sauce

Many chefs have recently put humble lamb shanks at center stage on their restaurant menus. Let them braise it for hours—with a pressure cooker, the home cook can prepare shanks in under an hour. This garlic sauce is a great way to accent the delectable meat.

½ teaspoon salt
¼ teaspoon dried rosemary
¼ teaspoon dried thyme
¼ teaspoon freshly ground black pepper
Four 1¼-pound lamb shanks
2 tablespoons extra-virgin olive oil
8 garlic cloves, crushed under a chef's knife
   and peeled
1 cup dry white wine
½ cup Homemade Beef Stock (page 14) or
   canned low-sodium broth

1. In a small bowl, rub the salt, rosemary, thyme, and pepper between your fingertips to crush the herbs (or use a mortar and pestle). Sprinkle all over the shanks.

2. In a 5- to 7-quart pressure cooker, heat 1 tablespoon of the oil over medium-high heat. In batches, add the shanks and cook, turning occasionally, until lightly browned, about 3 minutes. Transfer the shanks to a plate and set aside.

3. Remove the cooker from the heat to cool slightly. Return to medium heat. Add the remaining 1 tablespoon oil and the garlic. Stir until the garlic is barely beginning to color, about 1 minute. Immediately add the wine. Bring to a boil, scraping up the browned bits on the bottom of the cooker with a wooden spoon. Add the stock. Return the shanks to the cooker.

4. Lock the lid in place. Bring to high pressure over high heat. Adjust the heat to maintain the pressure. Cook for 20 minutes. Remove from the heat and quick-release the pressure. Open the lid, tilting it away from you to block any escaping steam. Switch the positions of the shanks from top to bottom. Cover again, bring to high pressure, and cook for an additional 20 minutes. Transfer the shanks to a serving platter and cover with aluminum foil to keep warm.

5. Let the cooking liquid stand for about 5 minutes. Skim off any fat from the surface. Uncovered, bring to a boil over high heat. Cook, uncovered, until the liquid is evaporated by about half, about 5 minutes, whisking occasionally to help dissolve the garlic. Pour the sauce over the shanks and serve immediately.

——————

Makes 4 servings
Two 20-minute periods at high pressure

abilene **beef** and **bean chili**

There is a chili recipe for every cook in Texas. Some folks top their chili with shredded cheese, onions, and sour cream, but others think that kind of behavior should be reserved for an ice cream sundae, and want their chili naked. Beans are even more controversial: Some like them, yet some wouldn't be caught dead with legumes in their pot. One thing for sure: Most agree that tomatoes don't belong anywhere near the chili.

Base your decisions on your mood and what's in the cupboard. Cooking the beans with the meat often ends up with one of the two being under- or over-cooked. To play it safe, cook them separately, and stir them together at the end.

> 2 tablespoons olive oil, plus more as needed
> 2 pounds beef bottom round, cut into 1½-inch pieces
> 1 large onion, chopped
> 1 medium red bell pepper, seeded and chopped
> 1 jalapeño chile, seeded and finely chopped
> 3 garlic cloves, finely chopped
> 2 tablespoons chili powder
> ½ teaspoon salt, plus more to taste
> 2 cups Homemade Beef Stock (page 14) or canned low-sodium broth
> ¼ cup yellow cornmeal
> 1½ cups (12 ounces) dried pinto beans, soaked, drained, and cooked (see page 72), or two 15-ounce cans pinto beans, rinsed and drained

1. In a 5- to 7-quart pressure cooker, heat 1 tablespoon of the oil over medium-high heat. In batches, add the beef and cook, adding more oil as needed, turning occasionally, until browned, about 4 minutes. Transfer to a plate and set aside.

2. Pour out any fat in the cooker. Add the remaining 1 tablespoon oil and heat. Add the onion, red pepper, jalapeño, and garlic. Cook, stirring often, until the vegetables begin to soften, about 2 minutes. Add the reserved beef and any juices from the plate, and sprinkle with the chili powder and salt. Mix well. Stir in the stock, scraping up any browned bits on the bottom of the cooker.

3. Lock the lid in place. Bring to high pressure over high heat. Adjust the temperature to maintain the heat. Cook for 20 minutes. Remove from the heat and quick-release the pressure. Open the lid, tilting it away from you to block any escaping steam. Let the chili stand for 5 minutes.

4. Skim any fat from the surface of the chili. In a small bowl, whisk about 1 cup of the cooking liquid into the cornmeal to make a paste. Stir the cornmeal mixture into the chili, and add the beans. Cook, stirring often, until the juices are thickened, 3 to 5 minutes, taking care that the chili doesn't stick and scorch on the bottom of the cooker. Season with additional salt to taste. Serve immediately.

Makes 8 servings
20 minutes at high pressure

old-fashioned **beef** stew with carrots and potatoes

While all cooks have their own way to make beef stew, this one has the makings of an American classic. It is simply flavored with thyme and bay leaf, chunky with beef, carrots, and potatoes (substitute parsnips or turnips, if you like, or add other vegetables), and served with a rich brown sauce.

> 2 tablespoons vegetable oil, plus more as needed
> 2½ pounds beef chuck roast, cut into 1½-inch pieces
> ½ teaspoon salt, plus more to taste
> ¼ teaspoon freshly ground black pepper, plus more to taste
> 1 large onion, chopped
> 2 garlic cloves, finely chopped
> 2 cups Homemade Beef Stock (page 14) or canned low-sodium broth
> 1 tablespoon tomato paste
> ½ teaspoon dried thyme
> 1 bay leaf
> 4 medium carrots, cut into 1-inch lengths
> 4 medium (1 pound) red-skinned potatoes, scrubbed, cut into 1-inch pieces
> 3 tablespoons unsalted butter, at room temperature
> 3 tablespoons all-purpose flour

1. In a 5- to 7-quart pressure cooker, heat 1 tablespoon of the oil over medium-high heat. In batches, adding more oil as needed, add the beef and cook, turning occasionally, until browned, about 4 minutes. Transfer the beef to a plate. Season the beef with ½ teaspoon salt and ¼ teaspoon pepper and set aside. Pour off the fat in the cooker.

2. Add the remaining 1 tablespoon oil to the cooker and heat over medium heat. Add the onion and garlic. Cook, stirring occasionally, until the onion begins to soften, about 2 minutes. Stir in the stock, tomato paste, thyme, and bay leaf. Return the beef and any juices on the plate to the cooker.

3. Lock the lid in place. Bring to high pressure over high heat. Adjust the heat to maintain the pressure. Cook for 20 minutes. Remove from the heat and quick-release the pressure. Open the lid, tilting it away from you to block any escaping steam. Let the stew stand for 5 minutes.

4. Skim off any fat from the surface of the cooking liquid. Add the carrots and potatoes. Replace the lid and bring the stew back to high pressure over high heat. Cook for 5 minutes. Remove from the heat, quick-release the pressure, and remove the lid. Using a large skimmer or slotted spoon, transfer the meat and vegetables to a deep serving bowl and cover with aluminum foil to keep warm.

5. Bring the cooking liquid, uncovered, back to a boil over medium-high heat. In a medium bowl, using a rubber spatula, work the butter and flour together until smooth. Gradually whisk about 1 cup of the cooking liquid into the flour mixture to make a thin paste. Briskly whisk into the boiling liquid. Cook, stirring occasionally, until the sauce is thickened and no trace of raw flour taste remains, about 5 minutes. Season with additional salt and pepper. Pour the sauce over the meat and vegetables, stir gently, and serve.

Makes 6 servings
20 minutes at high pressure for meat,
then 5 minutes at high pressure for vegetables

cuban pot roast with capers and olives

Because the strips of vegetables look like tattered fabric, this is often called *ropa vieja,* Spanish for "old clothes." That's an impoverished name for a dish that tastes like a million bucks. Serve spooned over rice that has been cooked with a generous pinch of saffron in the cooking liquid.

1 tablespoon vegetable oil
2 pounds (¾-inch thick) beef chuck steaks, cut into 4 or 6 pieces to fit the cooker
½ teaspoon salt
¼ teaspoon freshly ground black pepper
1 medium onion, cut into ½-inch-thick half-moons
1 medium carrot, cut into ½-inch-thick rounds
1 medium red bell pepper, seeded, cut into ½-inch-thick strips
2 garlic cloves, finely chopped
One 28-ounce can tomatoes in juice, drained and chopped
1 cup Homemade Beef Stock (page 14) or canned low-sodium broth
½ teaspoon dried oregano
Pinch of cinnamon
¼ cup chopped pimiento-stuffed green olives
2 tablespoons bottled capers, rinsed

1. In a 5- to 7-quart pressure cooker, heat the oil over medium heat. In batches, add the beef and cook, turning once, until browned on both sides, about 4 minutes. Transfer to a plate. Season with the salt and pepper and set aside.

2. Add the onion, carrot, red pepper, and garlic to the cooker. Cook, stirring often, until the vegetables begin to soften, about 2 minutes. Add the tomatoes, stock, oregano, and cinnamon, stirring to scrape up any browned bits on the bottom of the cooker. Return the beef and any juices on the plate to the cooker.

3. Lock the lid in place. Bring to high pressure over high heat. Adjust the heat to maintain the pressure. Cook for 20 minutes. Remove from the heat and quick-release the pressure. Open the lid, tilting it away from you to block any escaping steam. Transfer the meat to a serving platter and cover with aluminum foil to keep warm.

4. Let the cooking liquid stand for about 5 minutes. Skim off any fat from the surface of the cooking liquid. Add the olives and capers. Cook, uncovered, over high heat, until the mixture is slightly thickened, 3 to 5 minutes. Pour over the meat and serve immediately.

Makes 4 to 6 servings
20 minutes at high pressure

pot roast à la française

When you say *pot-au-feu* in France, it means much more than pot roast, or even its literal translation of "pot on the fire." The beef and vegetables are simmered until tender, but they are reserved until the cooking broth is bolstered with pasta and served as a light first course. Admittedly, *pot-au-feu* usually contains more than one cut of beef, along with sausages, chicken, and just about whatever else you can fit into a huge stockpot. In the pressure cooker's case, the limitation of size just means that the dish is more accessible to the American palate. Serve the roast in the French style, with coarse salt, freshly ground black pepper, and Dijon mustard. This is one dish that is much better when prepared with homemade beef broth, as the cooking broth must be delicious.

1 tablespoon vegetable oil
One 3½-pound beef bottom round roast, tied
½ teaspoon salt, plus more to taste
¼ teaspoon freshly ground black pepper, plus more to taste
3 cups Homemade Beef Stock (page 14) or high-quality frozen beef stock (available at some supermarkets, and specialty grocers)
1 pound red-skinned potatoes, cut into 1-inch pieces
2 medium carrots, cut into 1-inch lengths
2 medium parsnips, cut into 1-inch lengths
⅓ cup small pasta, such as ditalini, cooked
2 tablespoons chopped parsley, for garnish
Freshly grated Parmesan cheese, for serving the broth
Coarse salt, freshly ground black pepper, and Dijon mustard, for serving

1. In a 5- to 7-quart pressure cooker, heat the oil over medium-high heat. Season the beef with ½ teaspoon salt and ¼ teaspoon pepper. Place in the pressure cooker and brown on all sides, about 5 minutes. Transfer the beef to a plate. Pour off any fat in the pot. Return the beef to the pot and pour in the stock.

2. Lock the lid in place. Bring to high pressure over high heat. Adjust the heat to maintain the pressure. Cook for 1¼ hours.

3. Meanwhile, preheat the oven to 200°F. Remove the pressure cooker from the heat and quick-release the pressure. Open the lid, tilting it away from you to block any escaping steam. Using a slotted spoon, transfer the beef and a ladleful of the cooking liquid to a deep, heat-proof serving bowl. Cover tightly with aluminum foil and keep warm in the oven.

4. Skim any fat from the surface of the cooking liquid. Add the potatoes, carrots, and parsnips to the pot. Lock the lid in place. Bring to high pressure over high heat. Cook for 5 minutes. Remove from the heat and quick-release the pressure. Using the slotted spoon, transfer the vegetables to the platter with the beef, cover, and return to the oven to keep warm.

5. Stir the cooked pasta and parsley into the broth. Season with additional salt and pepper. Serve hot in soup bowls, passing the Parmesan on the side.

6. To serve the meat and vegetables, transfer the roast to a carving board. Remove the strings and carve the meat. Return to the bowl and serve immediately, with the salt, pepper, and mustard.

Makes 6 to 8 servings
1¼ hours at high pressure for the meat,
then 5 minutes at high pressure for the vegetables

yankee pot roast

A basic pot roast recipe with clear-eyed, Yankee simplicity that can be embellished with vegetables or herbs, if you wish. Serve it with mashed potatoes.

1 tablespoon vegetable oil
One 3-pound rump roast, trimmed, but leaving the fat "cap" intact
½ teaspoon salt, plus more to taste
¼ teaspoon freshly ground black pepper, plus more to taste
1 medium onion, sliced into ¼-inch-thick half-moons
2 bay leaves
2 cups Homemade Beef Stock (page 14), canned low-sodium broth, or water
2 tablespoons unsalted butter, at room temperature
2 tablespoons all-purpose flour

1. In a 5- to 7-quart pressure cooker, heat the oil over medium-high heat. Season the roast with ½ teaspoon salt and ¼ teaspoon pepper. Add the roast to the pressure cooker, fat side down. Cook, turning occasionally, until browned on all sides, about 6 minutes. Transfer the roast to a plate. Pour off all but 1 tablespoon of the fat from the pot. Add the onion and cook until softened, about 3 minutes. Add the bay leaves.

2. Pour in the stock, scraping up any browned bits on the bottom of the pot with a wooden spoon. Return the roast to the pot. Lock the lid in place. Bring to high pressure over high heat. Adjust the heat to maintain the pressure. Cook for 1 hour.

Remove from the heat and quick-release the steam. Open the lid, tilting it away from you to block any escaping steam. Transfer the roast to a serving platter and cover loosely with foil to keep warm.

3. Remove the bay leaves from the cooking liquid and let the liquid stand for 5 minutes. Skim the fat from the top of the cooking liquid. In a small bowl, using a rubber spatula, work the butter and flour together until smooth. Whisk 1 cup of the cooking liquid into the butter/flour mixture to make a thin paste. Return the uncovered pot to the stove and bring the skimmed cooking liquid to a boil over medium heat. Whisk in the paste and cook until the liquid reduces slightly and thickens into a light-bodied gravy, about 6 minutes. Season with additional salt and pepper.

4. Slice the roast. Pour about half of the gravy over the meat. Pour the remaining sauce in a sauceboat and pass with the meat.

▬▬▬▬▬▬

Makes 6 servings
1 hour at high pressure

corned beef **boiled dinner**

I f there's one day of the year when corned beef and cabbage makes an appearance, it is, of course, St. Patrick's Day. But, if the holiday falls on a weekday, most cooks are hard-pressed to cook the traditional meal—it just takes too long! With a pressure cooker, the cooking time is more than cut in half. This is not your typical ho-hum boiled dinner; beer and spices give the cooking liquid a delicious depth of flavor. Serve with mustard and prepared horseradish sauce.

> One 3-pound corned beef brisket with pickling spice packet (see Note)
> 2 cups water
> One 12-ounce bottle of lager beer
> 2 medium onions, peeled and cut in half lengthwise
> 2 garlic cloves, peeled and crushed
> 4 medium (1 pound) red-skinned potatoes, scrubbed but unpeeled, cut into 1-inch pieces
> 4 medium carrots, cut into 1-inch lengths
> 1 small (2 pounds) head green cabbage, cut into 6 wedges

1. Rinse the corned beef, but do not trim the fat. Tie the spices in a double thickness of cheesecloth.

2. Place the rack in a 5- to 7-quart pressure cooker. Add the water, beer, onions, garlic, and spice sachet. Place the corned beef in the pot (don't worry if it touches the sides—it will shrink during cooking).

3. Lock the lid in place. Bring to high pressure over high heat. Adjust the heat to maintain the pressure. Cook for 1 hour, 10 minutes. Let the steam release naturally (about 15 minutes). Open the lid, tilting it away from you to block any escaping steam.

4. Transfer the meat to a serving platter. Using a slotted spoon, transfer the onions to a large serving bowl. Cover both with aluminum foil to keep warm.

5. Place the potatoes and carrots in the cooking liquid in the pot. (The nitrates in the corned beef will probably have turned the liquid red, but don't be concerned.) Place the cabbage on top, trying to sub-merge it in the broth as much as possible. Lock the lid in place. Bring to high pressure over high heat. Adjust the heat to maintain the pressure. Cook for 6 minutes. Using a mesh skimmer or slotted spoon, transfer the vegetables to the serving bowl.

6. Slice the corned beef across the grain. Serve, with the vegetables passed on the side.

Note: Most corned beef comes packaged with a separate packet of pickling spices. If yours doesn't, substitute ½ teaspoon yellow mustard seeds, ½ teaspoon whole black peppercorns, 6 whole allspice berries, 6 whole cloves, and 1 crumbled bay leaf. If your corned beef is coated with spices, rinse them off under cold running water, as the free-floating spices could clog the vent.

Makes 4 to 6 servings
1 hour, 10 minutes at high pressure for the beef,
then 6 minutes at high pressure for the vegetables

beef brisket with onion-raisin sauce

Long-cooked beef brisket is a real treat, but it can take hours. Until the pressure cooker came into our lives, we cooked it only occasionally. Now it offers one of the easiest ways to get dinner on the table, and in much less time. Try this as a sandwich—thinly slice the brisket and serve it on soft buns, with the onion-raisin sauce spooned on top.

1 tablespoon vegetable oil
3 medium onions, cut into ½-inch-wide half-moons
4 medium carrots, cut into ½-inch rounds
½ cup raisins
½ cup Homemade Beef Stock (page 14) or canned low-sodium beef broth (see Note)
2 tablespoons cider vinegar
2 tablespoons light brown sugar
1 bay leaf
One 3-pound first-cut beef brisket, trimmed
½ teaspoon salt
½ teaspoon freshly ground black pepper

1. In a 5- to 7-quart pressure cooker, heat the oil over medium heat. Add the onions and carrots and cook until the vegetables begin to soften, about 2 minutes. Stir in the raisins, stock, vinegar, brown sugar, and bay leaf. Season the brisket with the salt and pepper. Place the brisket in the pot (it may touch the sides, but that's fine).

2. Lock the lid in place. Bring to high pressure over high heat. Adjust the heat to maintain high pressure. Cook for 1 hour. Let the steam release naturally (allow about 15 minutes). Open the lid, tilting it away from you to block any escaping steam.

3. Transfer the brisket to a serving platter and cover with foil to keep warm. Skim any fat from the surface of the cooking liquid. Bring to a boil over high heat. Cook, uncovered, until the liquid is reduced by about half, about 5 minutes. Discard the bay leaf. Pour the sauce into a bowl.

4. Thinly slice the brisket across the grain. Serve with the onion-raisin sauce.

Note: If needed, add more stock to meet your cooker's minimum liquid requirement. Boil the cooking liquid as needed to reduce to sauce consistency.

Makes 4 to 6 servings
1 hour at high pressure

deviled short ribs

Short ribs are surely one of the most succulent ways to enjoy beef. Our recipe renders out their fat, leaving it behind in the cooking liquid. (You won't use the liquid in this dish, but it should be reserved and used as beef broth at another meal.) The ribs are spread with spicy mustard, coated with crumbs, and baked quickly to give them a crunchy crust. Hold out on making this dish until you find meaty short ribs—some butchers put out ribs that Fido might like, but don't have enough meat on them for hungry humans.

2 tablespoons olive oil
4 pounds meaty beef short ribs
¼ teaspoon salt
1 medium onion, chopped
1 medium carrot, chopped
3 garlic cloves, crushed under a knife and peeled
2 cups water
¼ teaspoon dried thyme
¼ teaspoon whole black peppercorns
1 bay leaf

Nonstick cooking oil spray

DEVILED CRUST
6 tablespoons Dijon mustard
1 garlic clove, crushed through a press
⅛ teaspoon ground hot red pepper flakes
2 cups fresh Italian or French bread crumbs
   (make in a blender or food processor)
2 tablespoons olive oil

1. In a 5- to 7-quart pressure cooker, heat 1 tablespoon of the oil over medium-high heat. In batches, add the short ribs and cook, turning occasionally, until lightly browned, about 3 minutes. Transfer the ribs to a plate, season with the salt, and set aside.

2. Pour off any fat in the cooker. Return the cooker to medium heat. Add the remaining 1 tablespoon oil. Add the onion, carrot, and garlic. Cook, stirring often, until the vegetables begin to soften, about 2 minutes. Add the water, scraping up the browned bits on the bottom of the cooker with a wooden spoon. Add the thyme, peppercorns, and bay leaf. Return the ribs to the cooker.

3. Lock the lid in place. Bring to high pressure over high heat. Adjust the heat to maintain the pressure. Cook for 20 minutes. Remove from the heat and quick-release the pressure. Open the lid, tilting it away from you to block any escaping steam. Switch the positions of the ribs from top to bottom. Cover again, bring to high pressure, and cook for an additional 20 minutes.

4. Meanwhile, preheat the oven to 400°F. Line a baking sheet with aluminum foil and spray with the cooking oil.

5. Remove the pot from the heat and quick-release the pressure. Open the lid, tilting it away from you to block any escaping steam. Transfer the short ribs to a wire rack set over a jelly-roll pan and let drain. Pat the ribs dry with paper towels. (The ribs can be prepared up to this point 1 hour ahead and stored, loosely covered with aluminum foil, at room temperature. If desired, strain the cooking liquid and cool to room

temperature. Refrigerate overnight, and remove the hardened fat on the surface. Use as beef broth.)

6. To make the deviled crust: In a small bowl, mix the mustard, garlic, and hot pepper. Mix the bread crumbs and olive oil in a shallow dish until the crumbs are evenly moistened. Brush the meaty part of the ribs with the mustard mixture and roll in the bread crumbs. Place on the prepared baking sheet. Bake, turning once, until the crust is lightly browned, 10 to 15 minutes. Serve hot.

━━━━━━━━━━

Makes 4 servings
Two 20-minute periods

sweet-and-spicy **barbecued** country **ribs**

This is the recipe to make when you hanker for finger-licking ribs, but you don't want to crank up the outdoor grill. Our two-step pressure-cook-and-glaze procedure ensures great results. We prefer meaty country ribs to spareribs for this recipe. Serve it with cornbread and coleslaw for a delicious down-home meal.

    1 tablespoon vegetable oil
    3 pounds country pork ribs, cut into individual
      ribs (8 ribs)
    ½ teaspoon salt
    ¼ teaspoon freshly ground black pepper
    1 medium onion, chopped
    2 garlic cloves, minced
    1 cup catsup
    ½ cup jalapeño jelly or apricot preserves
    2 teaspoons chili powder
    ½ cup water

1. In a 5- to 7-quart pressure cooker, heat the oil over medium-high heat. In batches, add the ribs and brown lightly, about 5 minutes. Transfer to a plate, season with the salt and pepper, and set aside.

2. Pour out all but 1 tablespoon of the fat in the pot. Add the onion and garlic and cook until barely softened, about 1 minute. Stir in the catsup, jelly, chili powder, and water. Return the ribs to the pot.

3. Lock the lid in place. Bring to high pressure over high heat. Adjust the heat to maintain the pressure. Cook for 25 minutes. Remove from the heat and quick-release the pressure. Open the lid, tilting it away from you to block any escaping steam. Transfer the ribs to a platter and cover with foil to keep warm.

4. Position a rack 6 inches from the source of heat and preheat the broiler. Lightly oil the broiler rack.

5. While the broiler is heating, let the cooking liquid stand for 3 minutes. Skim off the fat that rises to the top. Bring to a boil over high heat. Cook, uncovered, stirring often, until thickened and reduced to about 2 cups, about 12 minutes.

6. Arrange the ribs on the prepared broiler rack. Brush with some sauce. Broil until glazed, about 2 minutes. Turn, brush with more sauce, and broil until the other side is glazed, about 2 minutes. Serve immediately, with the remaining sauce on the side.

———

Makes 4 servings
25 minutes at high pressure

pork chops with cherry—black currant sauce

Arlene adapted this recipe from *The Silver Palate Cookbook*. We've added some brown sugar to balance the tart flavors (add it to taste, because the sweetness varies with each brand of currant preserves) and some dried cherries for texture. When choosing pork loin chops for the pressure cooker, ask for the ones closer to the rib section. They will be slightly less lean and with more muscle separations, but they will not dry out as easily as center-cut chops. The timing is very precise, so have the timer set and ready to activate as soon as the pot reaches pressure.

- ¼ **cup dried cherries or cranberries**
- 1 **tablespoon vegetable oil**
- Six 8-ounce pork loin chops, cut 1 inch thick from the rib end, well trimmed of excess fat
- ¼ **teaspoon salt, plus more to taste**
- ⅛ **teaspoon freshly ground black pepper, plus more to taste**
- ¼ **cup high-quality black currant preserves**
- 1½ **tablespoons Dijon mustard**
- ⅓ **cup white wine vinegar**
- 2 **tablespoons light brown sugar**

1. Preheat the oven to 200°F. In a small bowl, soak the dried cherries or cranberries in warm water to cover until plumped, about 10 minutes. Drain.

2. In a 5- to 7-quart pressure cooker, heat the oil over medium-high heat. Lightly season the pork chops with ¼ teaspoon salt and ⅛ teaspoon pepper. In batches, place in the pot and cook, turning once, until browned on both sides, about 3 minutes. Transfer to a plate.

3. Meanwhile, in a small bowl, mix the preserves and mustard. Return the chops to the pot, slathering the top of each one with the preserve mixture. Lock the lid in place. Bring to high pressure over high heat. Adjust the heat to maintain the temperature. Cook for 1 minute, 15 seconds. Remove from the heat and quick-release the pressure. Open the lid, tilting it away from you to block any escaping steam. Transfer the pork chops to a platter, cover loosely with foil, and keep warm in the oven while making the sauce.

4. Using a wooden spoon, stir the vinegar and brown sugar into the pot, scraping up any browned bits from the bottom and sides of the pan. Cook, uncovered, until the sauce is thickened and reduced by about half, 3 to 5 minutes. Pour any juices from the chops into the sauce and boil for a few seconds. Season with additional salt and pepper. Pour the sauce over the pork chops and serve immediately.

▬▬▬▬▬

Makes 4 servings
1 minute, 15 seconds at high pressure

pork and winter squash stew with sage

The success of this autumnal stew depends on the cut of pork. Boneless pork shoulder cubes are sometimes available at the butcher, but it's more reliable to cut up your own roast. Whole pork shoulders (also called *pernil* or *calas* at Latino markets) are inexpensive, because there is a fair amount of loss from trimming the fat and skin—a 5-pound shoulder will yield about 2½ pounds of meat after trimming. Even so, pork shoulders are good buys. Serve with bulgur, the nutty flavor of which is the perfect foil for this stew.

    2 tablespoons vegetable oil
    2½ pounds boneless pork shoulder, cut into 1½-
        inch cubes
    ½ teaspoon salt, plus more to taste
    ¼ teaspoon freshly ground black pepper, plus
        more to taste
    4 medium carrots, cut into 1-inch lengths
    1 cup chopped leeks, white and pale green parts only
    1 medium red bell pepper, seeded and chopped
    2 garlic cloves, minced
    ⅓ cup dry sherry
    1 tablespoon red wine vinegar
    1½ cups Homemade Chicken Stock (page 13)
        or canned low-sodium broth
    One medium (1¾ pounds) butternut squash,
        peeled, seeded, and cut into 1-inch cubes
    2 tablespoons cold water
    1½ tablespoons cornstarch
    1 tablespoon chopped fresh sage

1. In a 5- to 7-quart pressure cooker, heat 1 tablespoon of the oil over medium-high heat. In batches, add the pork and cook, turning occasionally, until lightly browned, about 4 minutes. Transfer to a plate, season with ½ teaspoon salt and ¼ teaspoon pepper, and set aside.

2. Add the remaining 1 tablespoon oil to the pot and return to medium heat. Add the carrots, leeks, red pepper, and garlic. Cook, stirring often, until the vegetables begin to soften, about 2 minutes. Add the sherry and vinegar and stir, scraping up the browned bits on the bottom of the pot with a wooden spoon. Stir in the stock. Return the pork and any juices on the plate to the pot.

3. Lock the lid in place. Bring to high pressure over high heat. Adjust the heat to maintain the pressure. Cook for 25 minutes. Remove from the heat and quick-release the pressure. Open the lid, tilting it away from you to block any escaping steam. Add the squash. Lock the lid in place again and bring to high pressure over high heat. Cook for 1 minute. Remove from the heat and quick-release the pressure. Open the lid. Using a large skimmer or slotted spoon, transfer the meat and vegetables to a serving bowl.

4. Skim any fat from the surface of the cooking liquid. Return the cooker to medium heat and bring the liquid to a simmer. Place the water in a small bowl, sprinkle with the cornstarch, and stir to dissolve. Stir into the simmering liquid and cook until thickened. Stir in the sage. Season with additional salt and pepper. Pour the sauce over the stew, and serve hot.

Makes 6 servings
25 minutes at high pressure for the pork,
then 1 minute at high pressure for the squash

five-spice pork roast

This Asian-inspired roast is rubbed with five-spice powder (available at Asian grocers and many supermarkets) and cooked in a ginger-scented broth. Steam asparagus spears to serve on the side, along with rice to soak up the delicious sauce.

1 tablespoon vegetable oil
One 3-pound boneless center-cut pork loin, fat trimmed to ⅛ inch, tied
½ teaspoon five-spice powder
¼ teaspoon salt
1 scallion, white and green parts, coarsely chopped
2 tablespoons shredded fresh ginger (use the large holes on a box grater)
1 garlic clove, crushed under a knife and peeled
2 tablespoons dry sherry
1 cup Homemade Chicken Stock (page 13) or canned low-sodium broth
2 tablespoons Japanese soy sauce
1½ tablespoons cornstarch
Freshly ground black pepper, to taste
Chopped scallion greens, for garnish

1. In a 5- to 7-quart pressure cooker over medium-high heat, heat the oil. Add the pork roast and cook, turning occasionally, until lightly browned on all sides, about 4 minutes. Transfer the pork to a platter. In a small bowl, mix the five-spice powder and salt together, and season the pork with the mixture.

2. Add the scallion, ginger, and garlic to the pot. Stir over medium heat until fragrant, about 30 seconds. Add the sherry and stir well. Add the stock, stirring to scrape up the browned bits on the bottom of the pot with a wooden spoon. Return the pork to the pot.

3. Lock the lid in place. Bring to high pressure over high heat. Adjust the heat to maintain the pressure. Cook for 30 minutes. Remove from the heat and quick-release the pressure. Open the lid, tilting it away from you to block any escaping steam. Insert a meat thermometer in the center of the roast. It should read about 150°F. The temperature of the roast will rise another 5° to 10°F while standing. Transfer the roast to a serving platter and cover loosely with aluminum foil. Let the roast stand for 10 minutes before carving.

4. Let the cooking liquid stand for 5 minutes. Skim off any fat that rises to the surface. Return the cooking liquid to medium heat and bring to a boil, uncovered. Place the soy sauce in a small bowl, sprinkle with the cornstarch, and stir to dissolve. Stir into the boiling liquid and cook until thickened. Season the sauce with pepper.

5. Remove the strings and slice the roast. Arrange the roast on the platter and sprinkle with the scallions. Serve immediately, with the sauce passed on the side.

––––––––––

Makes 6 servings
30 minutes at high pressure

veal roast with prosciutto, sage, and lemon

Veal shoulder is a succulent cut of meat and one that takes especially well to pressure-cooking. A symbiotic trio of prosciutto, fresh sage, and lemon juice make this a delicious pot roast with only a few tablespoons of sauce, but that sauce will be packed with flavor. Tell the delicatessen counter not to slice the prosciutto too thin—it should not be paper-thin, or you won't be able to taste it. And don't trim off the prosciutto fat! It will melt into the lean veal and baste it from the inside.

One 2-pound veal shoulder roast
2 ounces sliced prosciutto
3 teaspoons chopped fresh sage
¼ teaspoon salt, plus more to taste
⅛ teaspoon freshly ground black pepper, plus more to taste
1 tablespoon olive oil
1 garlic clove, finely chopped
½ cup dry white wine, such as Pinot Grigio or Sauvignon Blanc
½ cup water
1 tablespoon fresh lemon juice, plus more to taste

1. Untie the roast and unroll it. Place the prosciutto over the surface of the veal, trimming the prosciutto to fit. Sprinkle with 1 teaspoon sage. Roll the roast up and tie crosswise with kitchen string at 2-inch intervals. Season with ¼ teaspoon salt and ⅛ teaspoon pepper.

2. In a 5- to 7-quart pressure cooker, heat the oil over medium-high heat. Add the veal and cook, turning occasionally, until lightly browned on all sides, about 4 minutes. Transfer the veal to a plate.

3. Add the garlic to the cooker and stir until fragrant, about 30 seconds. Do not brown. Add the wine and stir to release the browned bits on the bottom of the cooker. Stir in the water. Return the veal to the cooker.

4. Lock the lid in place. Bring to high pressure over high heat. Adjust the heat to maintain the pressure. Cook for 40 minutes. Remove from the heat and quick-release the pressure. Open the lid, tilting it away from you to block any escaping steam. Transfer the veal to a serving platter and cover loosely with foil to keep warm.

5. Skim any fat from the surface of the cooking liquid. Add the lemon juice and remaining 2 teaspoons sage. Bring to a boil over high heat. Boil, uncovered, until the liquid is thickened and evaporated by about half, about 6 minutes. Season with additional lemon juice, salt, and pepper.

6. Remove the string and carve the veal crosswise into thick slices. Serve, spooning the sauce over the veal.

Makes 6 servings
40 minutes at high pressure

osso bucco presto

One day while testing recipes for this book, Rick's friend Kelly Volpe was in the kitchen helping out. Rick served her a bowl of this tender, fragrant osso bucco, and for the rest of the afternoon, Kelly kept muttering, "I can't believe that osso bucco cooked for only 25 minutes!" These veal shanks are so good that you may find they don't even need the gremolata finish. Unfortunately, cross-cut veal shanks for osso bucco have become pricey, so you may have to save this recipe for company, or for payday. Choose the meatiest shanks—sometimes you get too much bone. The marrow is delectable, and should be spread onto bread and savored.

2 tablespoons olive oil
6 meaty veal shanks (3¼ pounds), cross-cut 1½ inches thick, tied with kitchen twine (see Note)
½ teaspoon salt
¼ teaspoon freshly ground black pepper
1 medium onion, chopped
1 medium carrot, cut into ½-inch dice
1 medium celery rib, cut into ½-inch dice
2 garlic cloves, minced
½ cup dry white wine
One 15-ounce can tomatoes in juice, drained and chopped, ½ cup tomato juice reserved
½ teaspoon dried basil
½ teaspoon dried rosemary

GREMOLATA
2 tablespoons chopped fresh parsley
Grated zest of 1 lemon
1 garlic clove, minced

1. In a 5- to 7-quart pressure cooker, heat 1 tablespoon of the oil over medium-high heat. In batches, add the veal shanks and cook, turning occasionally, until lightly browned, about 3 minutes. Transfer the veal to a platter and season with the salt and pepper.

2. Add the remaining 1 tablespoon oil to the pressure cooker and heat. Add the onion, carrot, celery, and garlic and cook, stirring occasionally, until softened, about 3 minutes. Stir in the wine and cook until almost evaporated. Add the tomatoes and the ½ cup tomato juice, basil, and rosemary. Return the veal to the pressure cooker.

3. Lock the lid in place. Bring to high pressure over high heat. Adjust the heat to maintain the pressure. Cook for 25 minutes.

4. Meanwhile, make the gremolata: In a small bowl, combine the parsley, lemon zest, and garlic. Set aside.

5. Remove the cooker from the heat and quick-release the pressure. Open the lid, tilting it away from you to block any escaping steam. Arrange the veal on a serving platter. Pour the tomato sauce over the veal. Sprinkle with the gremolata and serve immediately.

Note: If the butcher hasn't already done so, tie the shanks with kitchen twine to hold the meat in shape during cooking. Tie each piece of veal securely around its circumference. To hold the marrow in place, tie again over the top of the bone.

Makes 4 servings
25 minutes at high pressure

veal breast with white wine and herbs

Veal breast is beloved by European cooks, who prize its gelatinous, flavorful meat. It must be long-cooked to transform it from a tough piece of meat into one of the most tender, melt-in-your-mouth dishes around, and pressure cooking does this better and more quickly than any other method. Veal breast is sometimes boned and stuffed, but try it this way—unstuffed, with classic flavors of white wine, shallots, and herbs. It is wonderful served with oven-roasted potatoes.

> 2 tablespoons extra-virgin olive oil
> One 4-pound, 3-rib veal breast (see Note), trimmed
> ¼ teaspoon salt, plus more to taste
> ¼ teaspoon freshly ground black pepper, plus more to taste
> ¼ cup finely chopped shallot
> 1 garlic clove, minced
> ¼ cup dry white wine
> ½ cup Homemade Veal or Chicken Stock (pages 14 and 13) or canned low-sodium broth
> ¾ teaspoon dried thyme
> ¾ teaspoon dried rosemary

1. In a 5- to 7-quart pressure cooker, heat the oil over medium-high heat. Season the veal breast with ¼ teaspoon salt and ¼ teaspoon pepper. Place in the pot and brown on both sides, about 5 minutes. Transfer to a plate.

2. Add the shallot and garlic to the pot and cook, stirring often, until softened, about 1 minute. Add the wine and cook until almost completely reduced, about 1 minute. Stir in the stock. Return the veal breast to the pot, and sprinkle with the thyme and rosemary.

3. Lock the lid in place. Bring to high pressure over high heat. Adjust the heat to maintain the pressure. Cook for 1 hour. Remove from the heat and quick-release the pressure. Open the lid, tilting it away from you to block any escaping steam. Transfer the veal to a platter and cover with foil to keep warm.

4. Let the cooking liquid stand for 5 minutes. Skim off any fat from the surface. Bring to a boil, uncovered, over high heat. Cook, uncovered, until slightly reduced, about 5 minutes. Season the sauce with additional salt and pepper. Pour the sauce into a sauceboat.

5. Carve the veal breast and serve with the sauce passed on the side.

Note: Ask the butcher to cut the breast bones horizontally about 3 inches from the bottom of the roast (at the thin end), cutting just through the bones to the meat to create a "hinged" piece of meat and bone. The breast can now be folded at the hinge to fit into a 5- to 7-quart pressure cooker. (You may not have to ask the butcher to do this—in some Italian neighborhoods, it is done as a matter of course.)

———

Makes 3 to 4 servings
1 hour at high pressure

poultry
and seafood

No matter what method is used to prepare them, poultry and seafood should never be overcooked—and it takes a little special attention to avoid this problem in the pressure cooker. The cooking times may seem ridiculously short, but resist the temptation to add extra time until you stop the cooking and check for doneness.

Poultry remains one of America's most popular foods. When preparing chicken or turkey in a pressure cooker, we prefer to remove the skin. The main reason is aesthetic (the skin shrivels unattractively), but there are health benefits, too, as it greatly reduces the amount of fat in the dish. Almost every cook knows that there is a lot of fat lurking in the skin of chicken and turkey. Remove the poultry skin, and there goes one-third of the fat grams. When poultry with its skin is cooked in a pressure cooker, the skin releases so much fat into the cooking liquid that it is difficult to skim off the fat from the liquid before serving. Of course, it's almost impossible to take the skin off chicken wings, so we always remove them when cutting up a chicken.

Seafood, including fish and shellfish (except for some squid recipes), has relatively short cooking times. We usually grill or sauté our seafood in minutes, and we don't see much good in searching for ways to cook it in the pressure cooker. But there are times when a soothing, flavorful seafood stew really fills the bill. In that case, we press the pressure cooker into service to prepare a tasty base mixture, and add the seafood at the last minute, just to cook through.

tips for **poultry** and **seafood**

➤ Before cooking poultry, always remove as much skin as possible. In most dishes, skinned chicken on the bone will give the best results. But, if cooked properly, boneless skinless chicken, even breast meat, will be perfectly succulent in the pressure cooker.

➤ If the recipe calls for a whole chicken, it should be cut up into quarters (with the wings removed) to fit into the pot. A 4-pound chicken is the perfect weight to give good-sized portions that cook in 10 minutes. Depending on the appetites at the table, a 4-pound chicken will serve two to four people.

➤ Instead of buying chicken quarters, cut up the chicken yourself. This will give you the back portion, neck, giblets, and wings to turn into stock. Store the pieces in the freezer until you have enough to make a batch.

To cut a chicken into quarters, use a large sharp knife. Set aside the neck and giblets. Make a slit down the backbone—this loosens the skin and makes it easier to cut up the chicken. Cut off the wings at the shoulder joints. On one side of the chicken, make an incision in the skin near the hip joint to reveal the joint. Pull one leg quarter away from the body so the joint pops out of the socket, and cut off the leg quarter at the joint. Repeat with the other leg quarter to give you two leg/drumstick quarters.

Fold the back away from the body to break it, and cut off the back portion at the break. Cut down one side of the backbone on the carcass. Cut through the keel bone (the thin, flexible, cartilage-like bone that separates the two breast halves) to divide the breast in half lengthwise. The backbone will still be attached to one breast half; cut it off lengthwise. You will have two breasts and two leg quarters, and the back, backbone, neck, giblets, and wings for making stock or another use. Holding the skin with a paper towel, pull it off each breast. Repeat with the leg quarters, starting at the large end of the leg, pulling towards the drumstick, and cutting at the knee (don't worry about the little bit of skin left). Discard the skin.

Dark meat usually takes a bit longer to cook than white meat. Put the leg quarters in the cooker first, then the breasts. The legs in the cooking liquid will get a little extra cooking time as the liquid comes to a boil.

➤ Buy your fish on the bone, and ask the fish-
monger to fillet them for you. Take home the bones
and head to make Homemade Fish Stock (page 15).

➤ Homemade Fish Stock is delicious, but you
can substitute bottled clam juice, if you like.
Dilute the clam juice with equal portions of water,
or it could be too salty in the pressure cooker.

moroccan chicken with lemon and green olives

The exotic flavors of Moroccan cooking are just the thing to perk up a weeknight chicken supper. Use plump, full-flavored green olives from the delicatessen counter or a high-quality bottled variety. Couscous is the perfect partner for this dish.

½ teaspoon ground cumin
½ teaspoon ground ginger
½ teaspoon ground coriander
½ teaspoon salt
¼ teaspoon crushed hot red pepper flakes
One 4-pound chicken, quartered, skin removed (see page 58)
1 tablespoon olive oil
1 small onion, finely chopped
3 garlic cloves, finely chopped
1 cup Homemade Chicken Stock (page 13) or canned low-sodium broth
¼ cup fresh lemon juice
6 ounces Mediterranean green olives, pitted and coarsely chopped
2 tablespoons chopped fresh cilantro

1. In a small bowl, mix the cumin, ginger, coriander, salt, and red pepper. Rub the mixture all over the chicken. Set aside for 10 minutes.

2. In a 5- to 7-quart pressure cooker, heat the oil over medium-high heat. In batches, cook the chicken, turning once, until lightly browned on both sides, about 3 minutes. Transfer to a plate and set aside.

3. Add the onion and garlic and cook until the onion begins to soften, about 1 minute. Stir in the stock. Return the chicken to the cooker, leg quarters first, then the breast, meaty sides up. Lock the lid in place. Bring to high pressure over high heat. Adjust the heat to maintain the pressure. Cook for 10 minutes. Remove from the heat and quick-release the pressure. Open the lid, tilting it away from you to block any escaping steam. Transfer the chicken to a serving platter and cover with aluminum foil to keep warm.

4. Skim any fat from the surface of the cooking liquid. Stir the lemon juice and olives into the cooking liquid. Bring to a boil, uncovered, over medium-high heat. Cook until slightly thickened, about 5 minutes. Pour over the chicken and sprinkle with the cilantro. Serve hot.

Makes 2 to 4 servings
10 minutes at high pressure

bbq chicken

Arlene says that she remembers her mother making barbecue chicken in her pressure cooker during the pot's first big splash in the American kitchen in the forties and fifties. The old way had just two ingredients, chicken and bottled barbecue sauce. This recipe gives you an opportunity to use your favorite sauce, but most of them tend to scorch. Sidestep this problem by adding some water to the sauce. A quick glaze under the broiler gives a delectable finish. To complete the meal, serve with home-fried potatoes and a crisp salad.

1 tablespoon vegetable oil
1 medium onion, chopped
2 garlic cloves, chopped
½ cup prepared barbecue sauce
½ cup water
One 4-pound chicken, quartered, with skin removed (see page 58)
¼ teaspoon salt
⅛ teaspoon freshly ground black pepper

1. In a 5- to 7-quart pressure cooker, heat the oil over medium heat. Add the onion and garlic and cook until the vegetables soften, about 2 minutes. Stir in the barbecue sauce and water. Add the chicken, leg quarters first, then the breasts, meaty sides up.

2. Lock the lid in place. Bring to high pressure over high heat. Adjust the heat to maintain the pressure. Cook for 10 minutes. Quick-release the pressure. Open the lid, tilting it away from you to block any escaping steam. (Don't worry if the chicken looks a little pink at the bone, as it will continue to cook in the broiler.) Transfer the chicken to an oiled broiler rack. Season the chicken with the salt and pepper and set aside.

3. Position the broiler pan 6 inches from the source of heat and preheat the broiler. Meanwhile, bring the cooking liquid in the pot to a boil over medium-high heat. Cook uncovered, stirring often to avoid scorching, until the sauce thickens, about 5 minutes.

4. Brush the chicken with the sauce. Broil until glazed, 2 to 3 minutes. Turn, brush with additional sauce, and broil until the other side is glazed. Serve hot, with the additional sauce on the side.

Makes 2 to 4 servings
10 minutes at high pressure

mexican chicken in soft tacos

Here's a mildly spiced chicken, onion, and peppers mixture to roll up in warm tortillas for a very quick meal. You may use your favorite bottled salsa, but why not make fresh salsa while the chicken cooks? It will take only a few minutes, and the chunkiness of homemade salsa is a nice contrast to the meltingly tender chicken. If you have a few extra minutes, boil the cooking liquid down and stir into the chicken and vegetables—though not essential, it will give a bit of extra flavor.

1 tablespoon olive oil
1 medium onion, cut into ½-inch-thick half-moons
1 medium red bell pepper, seeded and cut into ½-inch-thick strips
1 jalapeño chile, seeded and minced
1 garlic clove, minced
½ teaspoon dried oregano
½ teaspoon ground cumin
½ cup water
6 boneless, skinless chicken thighs
¼ teaspoon salt
¼ teaspoon freshly ground black pepper
3 tablespoons chopped fresh cilantro (optional)

SALSA
8 ripe plum tomatoes, seeded and chopped into ½-inch dice (pulse in a food processor, if desired)
1 ripe avocado, pit removed, peeled, and chopped (optional)
2 tablespoons finely chopped onion
1 tablespoon fresh lime juice
1 jalapeño chile, seeded and minced
1 garlic clove, crushed through a press
¼ teaspoon salt

8 warmed flour tortillas, for serving

1. In a 5- to 7-quart pressure cooker, heat the oil over medium-high heat. Add the onion, red pepper, jalapeño, garlic, oregano, and cumin. Cook, stirring often, until the onion begins to soften, about 2 minutes. Stir in the water. Season the chicken with the salt and pepper. Add to the pot. Lock the lid in place. Bring to high pressure over high heat. Adjust the heat to maintain the pressure. Cook for 7 minutes.

2. Meanwhile, make the salsa: In a medium bowl, mix all of the ingredients and set aside at room temperature.

3. Remove the pressure cooker from the heat and quick-release the pressure. Open the lid, tilting it away from you to block any escaping steam. Transfer the chicken to a cutting board. Using a large knife, coarsely chop the chicken and transfer to a serving bowl. Using a slotted spoon, transfer the vegetables to the bowl. Stir in the cilantro, if desired. Cover with aluminum foil to keep warm.

4. If desired, return the uncovered pot to high heat. Boil the cooking liquid until evaporated to a few tablespoons, about 6 minutes. Stir into the chicken and vegetables.

5. To serve, spoon the chicken-and-vegetable mixture and the salsa into a tortilla, and roll up.

Makes 8 tacos
7 minutes at high pressure

chicken with **tarragon-mustard** sauce

This is a versatile dish that is easy enough for a weeknight meal, but special enough for company. Broccoli is the perfect green vegetable to go with the mustard sauce. Serve with hot cooked egg noodles to soak up every last drop.

½ teaspoon dried tarragon
½ teaspoon salt, plus more to taste
¼ teaspoon freshly ground black pepper, plus more to taste
One 4-pound chicken, quartered and skinned (see page 58)
1 tablespoon vegetable oil
1 tablespoon unsalted butter
⅓ cup chopped shallots
½ cup dry white wine
½ cup Homemade Chicken Stock (page 13), or use canned low-sodium broth
2 tablespoons heavy cream
1 tablespoon Dijon mustard
1 tablespoon cornstarch
2 tablespoons chopped fresh parsley, for garnish

1. In a small bowl, rub the tarragon, ½ teaspoon salt, and ¼ teaspoon pepper together with your fingertips to crumble the tarragon well. Sprinkle the mixture all over the chicken.

2. In a 5- to 7-quart pressure cooker, heat the oil over medium-high heat. In batches, cook the chicken, turning once, until lightly browned on both sides, about 3 minutes. Transfer to a plate and set aside.

3. Pour out any oil in the cooker. Add the butter and heat over medium heat. Add the shallots and stir until softened, about 1 minute. Add the wine and bring to a boil, scraping up any browned bits on the bottom of the cooker. Stir in the stock.

4. Return the chicken to the cooker, leg quarters first, then the breast, meaty sides up. Lock the lid in place. Bring to high pressure over high heat. Adjust the heat to maintain the pressure. Cook for 10 minutes. Remove from the heat and quick-release the pressure. Open the lid, tilting it away from you to block any escaping steam. Transfer the chicken to a serving platter and cover with aluminum foil to keep warm.

5. Skim any fat from the surface of the cooking liquid. Bring to a boil, uncovered, over medium heat. In a small bowl, combine the cream and mustard. Add the cornstarch and stir until it is completely dissolved. Stir into the boiling liquid and cook just until thickened. Season the sauce with additional salt and pepper. Pour over the chicken, sprinkle with parsley, and serve immediately.

Makes 2 to 4 servings
10 minutes at high pressure

north beach **cioppino**

In San Francisco's North Beach, this fragrant fish stew is served at every kind of restaurant, from countertop luncheonette to formal bastion of *la cucina Italiana*. (Portuguese and Italian fishermen hotly dispute the origin of cioppino, but because Italian immigrants own more restaurants than the Portuguese, they seem to have won the argument.) It is often made with cracked Dungeness crab, and even though it's delicious, the crab shells make the dish somewhat difficult to eat politely. Stir in shelled crabmeat just before serving—the hot broth will heat it through.

2 tablespoons olive oil
1 medium onion, chopped
1 medium red or green bell pepper, seeded and chopped
2 celery ribs with leaves, chopped
2 garlic cloves, finely chopped
½ cup hearty red wine, such as Zinfandel
2 cups Homemade Fish Stock (page 15) or 1 cup bottled clam juice and 1 cup water
One 28-ounce can tomatoes in juice, drained and chopped
2 tablespoons tomato paste
½ teaspoon dried oregano
½ teaspoon dried basil
1 bay leaf
¼ teaspoon salt
¼ teaspoon crushed hot red pepper flakes
12 ounces skinless cod fillet, cut into 1-inch pieces
8 ounces medium shrimp, peeled and deveined
8 ounces lump crabmeat, picked over for cartilage

1. In a 5- to 7-quart pressure cooker, heat the oil over medium-high heat. Add the onion, red or green pepper, celery, and garlic. Cook, stirring often, until the vegetables begin to soften, about 2 minutes. Add the wine and bring to a boil. Stir in the stock, tomatoes, tomato paste, oregano, basil, bay leaf, salt, and hot pepper.

2. Lock the lid in place. Bring to high pressure over high heat. Adjust the heat to maintain the pressure. Cook for 10 minutes. Remove from the heat and quick-release the pressure. Open the lid, tilting it away from you to block any escaping steam.

3. Return the cooker to medium heat. Bring the cooking liquid to a simmer over medium heat, uncovered. Add the cod and shrimp and simmer until the fish turns opaque, about 2 minutes. Do not overcook. Stir in the crabmeat and remove from the heat.

4. Serve immediately in deep soup bowls.

Makes 8 servings
10 minutes at high pressure

shrimp and sausage gumbo

Some folks might consider gumbo a rib-sticking soup. As it is certainly substantial enough to make a meal, we think of it as a light stew, and one that we make often for supper. This basic recipe is very versatile, and can be turned into chicken or fish gumbo with a few simple substitutions. One of the essential ingredients of gumbo is roux, traditionally a browned combination of fat and flour. By toasting the flour alone in a skillet, you'll get the flavor without the extra fat. Another must-have is okra, whose juices help thicken the gumbo. If you don't like okra, you can leave it out or substitute green beans, but the gumbo won't be as thick.

1 tablespoon oil

8 ounces andouille or other smoked sausage, such as kielbasa, cut into ¼-inch-thick rounds

1 medium onion, chopped

1 medium celery rib with leaves, chopped

1 medium red bell pepper, seeded and chopped

2 garlic cloves, finely chopped

2 teaspoons Cajun Seasoning (recipe follows)

1 bay leaf

½ teaspoon salt, plus more to taste

4 cups Homemade Chicken Stock (page 13) or canned low-sodium broth

One 14½-ounce can tomatoes in juice, drained and chopped, juices reserved

⅓ cup all-purpose flour

One 10-ounce box frozen okra

1 pound medium shrimp, peeled, deveined, and each cut lengthwise in half

2 cups long-grain rice, cooked according to package directions (about 4 cups cooked rice)

1. In a 5- to 7-quart pressure cooker, heat the oil over medium heat. Add the sausage and cook, stirring often, until lightly browned, about 5 minutes. Stir in the onion, celery, red pepper, and garlic. Cook, stirring occasionally, until the vegetables begin to soften, about 2 minutes. Stir in the Cajun Seasoning, bay leaf, and ½ teaspoon salt. Add the stock, tomatoes, and their juices.

2. Lock the lid in place. Bring to high pressure over high heat. Adjust the heat to maintain pressure. Cook for 8 minutes.

3. Meanwhile, in a medium nonstick skillet over medium heat, cook the flour, stirring often, until it is toasted and turns beige, about 5 minutes. Transfer the toasted flour to a bowl and set aside.

4. Remove the cooker from the heat and quick-release the pressure. Open the lid, tilting it away from you to block any escaping steam. Remove the bay leaf. Gradually whisk about 1¼ cups of the cooking liquid into the flour to make a thin paste. Stir the paste into the cooker. Add the okra. Cook, uncovered, occasionally stirring and breaking up the block of okra, until the okra is tender, about 10 minutes. Stir in the shrimp and cook just until it turns pink and firm, about 1 minute. Season with additional salt.

5. To serve, place a spoonful of hot rice in each bowl. Spoon the gumbo over the rice and serve immediately.

Cajun Seasoning: In a small bowl, combine 2 tablespoons paprika (preferably sweet Hungarian), 1 tablespoon each dried basil and dried thyme, 1 teaspoon each garlic powder and onion powder, ½ teaspoon freshly ground black pepper, and ¼ teaspoon cayenne pepper. Store in a tightly covered jar.

Filé Gumbo: If you wish, use filé powder (ground sassafras leaves) to thicken the gumbo. Delete the okra. Stir the flour mixture into the soup and simmer until lightly thickened and no trace of raw flour flavor remains, about 5 minutes. Remove the cooker from the heat. Gradually stir in enough filé powder to thicken the gumbo to desired consistency, about 1½ tablespoons. After adding the filé powder, do not cook the gumbo or freeze it—when simmered, filé powder makes the gumbo very gooey.

Snapper or Cod Gumbo: Substitute 2 cups bottled clam juice and 2 cups water for the chicken stock. Substitute 1½ pounds skinned snapper or cod fillets, cut into 1-inch cubes, for the shrimp. Simmer until the fish is opaque, about 3 minutes.

Chicken Gumbo: Delete the shrimp. Brown 1¼ pounds boneless, skinless chicken thighs to the cooker along with the sausage. When removing the bay leaf, transfer the chicken thighs to a cutting board and set aside while the okra is simmering. Cut the chicken into bite-sized pieces, and return to the gumbo just before serving.

Makes 8 to 12 servings
8 minutes at high pressure

tuna steaks in basque sweet pepper ragout

Piperade, a Basque ragout of meltingly tender sweet peppers with onions, garlic, and tomato, makes a great bed for thick tuna steaks. This is a fine recipe for the pressure-cooker skillet, because it's easiest to get the tuna steaks in and out of a shallow pan. If you are using a 5- to 7-quart cooker, sear the tuna steaks in a separate skillet, then transfer them to the sweet peppers for their brief final cooking. Another option is to separately grill or broil the steaks and serve them atop the ragout. Make some rice or couscous to go alongside, and you'll have a very fast and healthful meal.

> 2 tablespoons extra-virgin olive oil
> Four 6-ounce (1¼ inches thick) tuna steaks
> ½ teaspoon salt
> ¼ teaspoon freshly ground black pepper
> 1 large onion, cut into ¼-inch-thick half-moons
> 1 medium red bell pepper, seeded and cut into
>   ½-inch-thick strips
> 1 medium yellow bell pepper, seeded and cut into
>   ½-inch-thick strips
> 2 garlic cloves, finely chopped
> One 14½-ounce can tomatoes in juice, drained
>   and chopped
> ⅛ teaspoon crushed hot red pepper flakes
> ⅓ cup Mediterranean black olives, pitted and
>   coarsely chopped

1. In a 2½-quart pressure skillet or a large nonstick skillet, heat 1 tablespoon of the oil over high heat until very hot but not smoking. Season the tuna steaks with ¼ teaspoon salt and the black pepper. Cook, turning once, for 1 minute per side, to just sear the tuna. Transfer to a plate and set aside. Do not cover.

2. In the pressure skillet or a 5- to 7-quart pressure cooker, heat the remaining 1 tablespoon oil over medium heat. Add the onion, red and yellow peppers, and garlic. Cook, stirring often, until the vegetables begin to soften, about 3 minutes. Stir in the tomatoes, the remaining ¼ teaspoon salt, and the hot pepper.

3. Lock the lid in place. Bring to high pressure over high heat. Adjust the heat to maintain the pressure. Cook for 5 minutes. Remove from the heat and quick-release the pressure. Open the lid, tilting it away from you to block any escaping steam.

4. Stir in the olives. Return the tuna to the pressure skillet or cooker. Lock the lid in place and cook over medium heat for 2 minutes—the cooker does not have to return to pressure. The steaks will have an opaque cooked ring surrounding a very rare center; simmer, covered, to cook longer to greater doneness, if desired.

5. Spoon the ragout onto dinner plates and top each serving with a tuna steak. Serve immediately.

Makes 4 servings
5 minutes at high pressure

This creamy fish chowder can be made with any meaty, firm-fleshed fish such as cod or haddock. If you prefer, substitute shellfish for the fish—the soup is excellent with shrimp, shucked oysters, or a combination.

2 tablespoons unsalted butter
1 cup chopped leeks, white and pale green parts only
2 medium celery ribs with leaves, chopped
1 garlic clove, minced
½ cup dry white wine, such as Sauvignon Blanc
3 cups Homemade Fish Stock (see page 15), or 2 cups bottled clam juice and 1 cup water
¼ teaspoon dried thyme
¼ teaspoon fennel seed
¼ teaspoon salt, plus more to taste
⅛ teaspoon crushed hot red pepper flakes
4 medium (1 pound) red-skinned potatoes, scrubbed, cut into ½-inch dice
⅓ cup heavy cream
¼ teaspoon crumbled saffron threads
2 teaspoons cornstarch
1½ pounds skinless cod or haddock fillets, cut into 1-inch pieces
Chopped fresh parsley, for garnish

1. In a 5- to 7-quart pressure cooker, melt the butter over medium-high heat. Add the leeks, celery, and garlic. Cook, stirring occasionally, until the vegetables begin to soften, about 2 minutes. Add the wine and bring to a boil. Add the stock, thyme, fennel seed, ¼ teaspoon salt, and hot pepper.

2. Lock the lid in place. Bring to high pressure over high heat. Adjust the heat to maintain the pressure. Cook for 10 minutes. Remove from the heat and quick-release the pressure. Open the lid, tilting it away from you to block any escaping steam.

3. Return the cooker to the stove. Add the potatoes to the cooker. Lock the lid in place. Bring to high pressure over high heat and cook for 3 minutes. Quick-release the pressure and open the lid. Reduce the heat to medium.

4. In a small bowl, combine the cream and saffron. Sprinkle the cornstarch into the bowl and mix well to dissolve. Stir into the simmering broth. Add the cod or haddock and cook until the fish is opaque and the liquid is lightly thickened, about 2 minutes. Season with additional salt.

5. Serve immediately in deep soup bowls, sprinkling each serving with parsley.

———————————

Makes 6 servings
10 minutes at high pressure for base,
then 3 minutes at high pressure for potatoes

beans

Beans are being rediscovered for their earthy flavor and healthful profile. The soluble fiber in beans has been linked to lowering blood cholesterol. Combining beans with grains creates a complete protein with all the essential amino acids. (You'll see that most of these recipes are served over rice or some other grain.)

Even in a regular pot, cooking dried beans is never precise. The age and relative dryness of the beans greatly affect the cooking time. Because there are so many variables, cooking charts for the different beans can be frustrating. We think it is best to give yourself a very wide berth when cooking beans to be sure that they don't overcook into mush.

Beans should always be soaked before cooking to help soften the fibers and leach out some of the indigestible enzymes. Many people prefer to soak their beans for at least 4 hours or overnight, which helps the beans keep their shape during cooking.

However, to do this requires thinking ahead. To give more opportunity for spontaneity, the beans can also be quick-soaked in a pressure cooker, then drained and pressure-cooked again for a few minutes. Instead of pressure-cooking the beans until they're tender, you will have more control over the process if you release the pressure and finish cooking them uncovered at normal atmospheric pressure. You'll add only a few minutes' cooking time to the whole procedure, but your beans will be in better shape.

When cooking the beans for a soup or purée, the quest for the perfectly shaped bean isn't a problem. The beans in these dishes can be completely cooked at high pressure. If a few beans are broken up, no one will notice or care. But when you want tender, intact beans for a salad or to stir into a stew, you'll be glad you used the two-step procedure.

tips for **beans**

➤ Old beans take forever to cook. As the freshness of beans is so important, buy them from a source with a high turnover. At a supermarket, Latino brands are a good bet; you can also purchase fresh dried beans at a natural foods store.

➤ To soak dried beans in a bowl, rinse the beans in a sieve, sorting through them to remove any stones. Place in a large bowl. Add enough cold water to cover the beans by at least 2 inches. The ideal soaking time is 4 to 6 hours. After that, the beans can hydrate *too* much, making it difficult to pressure-cook them without their breaking up. (As a matter of convenience, you can soak the beans for up to 12 hours. These long-soaked beans are best for cooking into soups or purées. Some thick-skinned beans, such as soybeans and large lima beans, need overnight soaking to properly soften their skins. Most cookbooks say "overnight," but realistically speaking, you would probably soak them all day long while you're at work to cook them in the evening for dinner.) In warm weather, refrigerate the beans in their soaking liquid. Drain the beans and rinse under cold running water. The beans are now ready for further cooking.

➤ To quick-soak the beans in a pressure cooker (our preference), place the rinsed and sorted beans and cold water in a 5- to 7-quart pressure cooker. For 1 cup dried beans, use 3 cups water; for 1½ cups beans, use 4 cups water; and for 2 cups beans, 6 cups water. Bring to high pressure over high heat. Cook for 2 minutes. Remove from the heat and quick-release the steam. Open the lid, tilting it away from you to block any escaping steam. Drain and rinse the beans under cold running water. The beans are now ready to be cooked.

➤ Never cook or quick-soak more than 1 pound (about 2½ cups) of dried beans at a time in a pressure cooker.

➤ Do not add salt to the soaking water or initial cooking liquid for dried beans. Salt toughens the skins and lengthens the cooking time, sometimes to the point where the beans never cook. Acidic ingredients, such as tomatoes or wine, also toughen bean skins (except for thin-skinned lentils). Salting the beans during their final cooking (after they have softened sufficiently) improves their flavor. If the beans are tender, add salt to their cooking water, and let the beans cool in the salted liquid.

➤ Before giving the beans their final cooking, always drizzle 1 tablespoon vegetable or olive oil to the surface of the cooking liquid to help reduce foaming.

➤ If the cooking liquid sputters through the vent during the quick-release, let the cooker stand for a few minutes, then try again.

➤ If possible, cool the beans in their cooking liquid. This improves their flavor and texture.

➤ Save the cooking liquid from drained beans to use in soups.

➤ Cooked beans taste best if made a day ahead. Stored tightly covered in their cooking liquid, they can be refrigerated for up to 3 days.

➤ When you have a collection of leftover dried beans, combine them to make a favorite bean soup. (Don't use black beans, which will color the whole batch.) Cook the beans until all of them are tender, and don't worry if a few break up.

estimated pressure-cooking times for beans

These estimated times are for quick-soaked beans, pressure-cooked at high pressure, then quick-released. The beans are then simmered, uncovered, in their cooking liquid until tender.

Black (Turtle) . . . . .7 minutes
Black-Eyed Peas* . . . . .5 minutes
Cannellini . . . . .5 minutes
Cranberry . . . . .3 minutes
Garbanzos (Chickpeas) . . . . .18 minutes
Great Northern . . . . .3 minutes
Kidney, Red .7 minutes
Lentils* . . . . .4 minutes
Lima, Baby .2 minutes
Navy . . . . .7 minutes
Pink . . . . .7 minutes
Pinto . . . . .7 minutes
Red Beans .6 minutes

* Do not soak.

basic beans

The chart on page 73 gives estimated cooking times, but be flexible. For 1 cup dried beans, use 3 cups water or stock; for 1½ cups dried beans, use 4 cups; and for 2 cups dried beans, use 6 cups. Beans cook to about twice their dried volume. If desired, season the beans with one small onion (peeled and cut in half for easy removal), a few peeled garlic cloves (no need to remove them after cooking), a bay leaf, and/or ¼ teaspoon dried thyme.

1 cup dried beans, soaked, drained, and rinsed (see page 72)
3 cups water, Homemade Chicken Stock (page 13), or canned low-sodium broth
1 tablespoon vegetable or olive oil
Salt, to taste

1. Place the beans and water or stock in a 5- to 7-quart pressure cooker. Drizzle the oil over the water or stock. Bring to high pressure over high heat. Adjust the heat to maintain the pressure. Cook for the time indicated in the chart on page 73. Remove from the heat and quick-release the pressure.

2. Open the lid, tilting it away from you to block any escaping steam. Check the beans for doneness. If necessary, return the uncovered pot to medium-low heat, season with salt, and bring to a simmer. Cook, testing the beans occasionally, until tender.

3. If possible, cool the beans in their cooking liquid. Drain the beans, saving the cooking liquid to use in soups, if desired.

Makes about 2 cups cooked beans
Cooking time at high pressure depends on bean variety

black beans with chorizo

A little bit of chorizo, a hard, spicy smoked sausage, goes a long way to season a whole pot of beans. You'll find it at Latino markets. (Do not substitute loose-pack chorizo, which resembles ground pork sausage. If necessary, use pepperoni.) Serve the beans with a stack of warm corn or flour tortillas, or spoon over rice.

2 tablespoons olive oil
6 ounces hard chorizo sausage, cut into ½-inch dice
1 large onion, chopped
1 medium red bell pepper, seeded and chopped
1 jalapeño pepper, seeded and finely chopped
2 garlic cloves, finely chopped
2 teaspoons chili powder
½ teaspoon dried oregano
3 cups Homemade Chicken Stock (page 13) or canned low-sodium broth
1 pound dried black beans, soaked and drained (see page 72)
½ teaspoon salt
Salsa (page 62), for serving
Sour cream, for serving
Chopped fresh cilantro, for serving

1. In a 5- to 7-quart pressure cooker, heat 1 tablespoon of the oil over medium heat. Add the chorizo and cook, stirring often, until lightly browned, about 3 minutes. Add the onion, red pepper, jalapeño, and garlic. Cook, stirring often, until the vegetables begin to soften, about 2 minutes. Add the chili powder and oregano and stir until fragrant, about 30 seconds. Stir in the stock and beans. Drizzle the remaining 1 tablespoon oil over the cooking liquid.

2. Lock the lid in place. Bring to high pressure over high heat. Adjust the heat to maintain the pressure. Cook for 7 minutes. Remove from the heat and quick-release the pressure. Open the lid, tilting it away from you to block any escaping steam.

3. Return the cooker to medium heat, stir in the salt, and bring to a simmer. Cook until the beans are tender, mashing some of the beans into the broth to thicken as desired, about 5 minutes.

4. Serve immediately in bowls, with the salsa, sour cream, and cilantro passed on the side for topping.

_____

Makes 8 servings
7 minutes at high pressure

pinto bean salad with chile vinaigrette

This salad is always a hit at summer get-togethers. Bean salads soak up their dressing and usually need to be reseasoned with additional dressing before serving.

VINAIGRETTE
- ¼ cup fresh lime juice
- 2 jalapeño peppers, seeded and minced
- 1 garlic clove, peeled
- 2 teaspoons sugar
- ½ teaspoon salt
- ¼ teaspoon freshly ground black pepper
- 1 cup olive oil

- 1 pound dried pinto beans, cooked, drained, and rinsed (see Basic Beans, page 74)
- 2 medium red bell peppers, roasted and chopped (see Note)
- 4 medium celery ribs, chopped
- 2 cups fresh or thawed corn kernels
- 4 scallions, finely chopped
- Salt and freshly ground black pepper, to taste
- 4 ounces firm goat cheese, such as Bucheron, crumbled (optional)

1. To make the vinaigrette: In a blender, combine the lime juice, jalapeños, garlic, sugar, salt, and pepper. With the machine running, add the oil in a stream until the vinaigrette thickens.

2. In a large bowl, mix the pinto beans, roasted red peppers, celery, corn, and scallions. Toss with ¾ cup of the vinaigrette. Cover and refrigerate until chilled, at least 2 hours.

3. Toss with the remaining ¼ cup vinaigrette. Season with salt and pepper. Top with the cheese, if desired. Serve chilled.

Pinto and Green Bean Salad: Bring a medium saucepan of lightly salted water to a boil over high heat. Add 8 ounces green beans, cut into 1-inch lengths. Cook until crisp-tender, about 3 minutes. Drain and rinse under cold running water. Stir into the salad just before serving.

Note: To roast a red bell pepper, position a broiler rack about 6 inches from the source of heat and preheat the broiler. Cut off the top of the pepper, just below and including the stem, then cut off ½ inch from the bottom. Push out and discard the stem. Slit the pepper down the side, open it up, and cut out the ribs and seeds. Spread out the pepper, skin side up, and press on it to flatten. Broil, skin side up, until the skin is blackened and blistered, 5 to 10 minutes. Be careful not to burn a hole through the pepper—only the skin should blacken. (The flattened pepper can also be grilled over a hot charcoal fire or a gas grill heated to the high setting.) Using kitchen tongs, transfer to a plate and cover with aluminum foil. Let stand until cool enough to handle. Using a small knife, peel and scrape off the skin. Try not to rinse the pepper under cold running water unless absolutely necessary.

Makes 8 to 12 servings
4 minutes at high pressure

cilantro hummus

This is a tasty all-purpose bean spread for serving with crisp pita or baguette toasts as an hors d'oeuvre or to slather onto sandwiches. Substitute other beans for the garbanzo beans if you wish, or other herbs (white beans and sage are an especially good combination).

1 cup dried garbanzo beans (chickpeas), soaked
   and drained (see page 72)
2 garlic cloves, crushed under a knife and peeled
6 tablespoons extra-virgin olive oil
3 tablespoons fresh lemon juice
½ teaspoon crushed hot red pepper flakes
⅓ cup chopped fresh cilantro leaves
½ teaspoon salt
Chopped cilantro, for garnish (optional)

1. In a 5- to 7-quart pressure cooker, cook the garbanzo beans according to the directions on page 74. Let the beans cool in the cooking liquid. Drain the beans, reserving the cooking liquid.

2. In a food processor fitted with the metal blade, with the machine running, drop the garlic through the feed tube to chop. Add the beans, oil, lemon juice, and hot pepper. With the machine running, gradually pour in enough of the reserved cooking liquid to make a smooth purée, scraping down the sides of the bowl as needed. Add the cilantro leaves and pulse until blended. Season with the salt. Transfer to a serving bowl and sprinkle with the chopped cilantro, if desired. Serve at room temperature.

───────────

Makes about 2½ cups
18 minutes at high pressure

garbanzo bean and escarole stew

Another vegetarian main course for bean lovers. It can be made with vegetable stock, but there's really so much flavor from the beans and vegetables that water works just as well. Serve with crusty whole-wheat bread and a crisp green salad, and you're all set.

3 tablespoons extra-virgin olive oil
1 medium red onion, thinly sliced into half-moons
1 medium onion, thinly sliced into half-moons
4 garlic cloves, finely chopped
1 pound garbanzo beans (chickpeas), soaked and drained (see page 72)
6 cups water or canned low-sodium chicken broth
½ teaspoon crushed hot red pepper flakes
One 14½-ounce can tomatoes in juice, drained and chopped
1 teaspoon salt
1 large (1½ pounds) head escarole, well rinsed, torn into large pieces
Freshly grated Parmesan cheese, for serving

1. In a 5- to 7-quart pressure cooker, heat 2 tablespoons of the oil over medium-high heat. Add the onion and cook, stirring often, until golden, about 5 minutes. Add the garlic and stir until fragrant, about 1 minute.

2. Add the beans, water, and hot pepper. Drizzle with the remaining 1 tablespoon oil. Lock the lid in place. Bring to high pressure over high heat. Adjust the heat to maintain the pressure. Cook for 20 minutes. Remove from the heat and quick-release the pressure. Open the lid, tilting it away from you to block any steam.

3. Stir in the tomatoes and salt and bring to a boil, uncovered, over medium-high heat. Gradually stir in the escarole, letting the first batch wilt before adding more. Do not fill the cooker more than two-thirds full. Lock the lid in place and return to high pressure over high heat. Cook for 3 minutes. Remove from the heat, quick-release the pressure, and open the lid.

4. Return to a boil over medium heat, crushing some of the beans against the side of the cooker with a large spoon to thicken the liquid. Serve hot in bowls, with the cheese passed on the side.

Makes 8 servings
20 minutes at high pressure for the beans,
then 3 minutes at high pressure for the escarole

cranberry bean, bulgur, and vegetable chili

Here's a rib-sticking chili that is so satisfying you'll never miss the meat. The recipe shows how the beans are almost completely cooked before adding the salt and tomatoes; if added sooner, these ingredients would prevent the beans from softening. Not only does the bulgur thicken the cooking liquid, it combines with the beans to give this vegetarian meal complete protein.

3 tablespoons olive oil
1 large onion, chopped
2 medium carrots, cut into ½-inch-thick rounds
2 medium celery ribs, cut into ½-inch-thick pieces
1 medium red bell pepper, seeded and cut into ½-inch pieces
2 jalapeños, seeded and finely chopped
4 garlic cloves, finely chopped
1 tablespoon chili powder
1½ cups dried cranberry or pinto beans, soaked and drained (see page 72)
3 cups water
One 14½-ounce can tomatoes in juice, drained and chopped
1 cup fresh or thawed frozen corn
1 tablespoon tomato paste
½ teaspoon salt
¾ cup bulgur

1. In a 5- to 7-quart pressure cooker, heat 2 tablespoons of the oil over medium-high heat. Add the onion, carrots, celery, red pepper, jalapeños, and garlic. Cook uncovered, stirring often, until the vegetables are almost tender, about 5 minutes. Add the chili powder and stir until fragrant, about 15 seconds. Transfer the vegetables to a bowl and set aside.

2. Add the beans and water to the pressure cooker. Drizzle with the remaining 1 tablespoon oil. Lock the lid in place. Bring to high pressure over high heat. Adjust the heat to maintain the pressure. Cook for 5 minutes. Remove from the heat and quick-release the pressure. Open the lid, tilting it away from you to block the steam.

3. Stir in the reserved vegetables, tomatoes, corn, tomato paste, and salt. Lock the lid in place, bring back to high pressure over high heat, and adjust the heat to maintain the pressure. Cook for 5 minutes. Remove from the heat, quick-release the pressure, and open the lid.

4. Stir in the bulgur. Cook, uncovered, over medium-low heat until the bulgur is tender and the chili thickens, 3 to 5 minutes. Serve hot.

Makes 8 servings
5 minutes at high pressure for the beans,
then 5 minutes at high pressure for the vegetables

new orleans **red beans** and **rice**

To this day, red beans and rice is the Monday daily special in many New Orleans restaurants (and homes, too). This tradition started many years ago when Monday was laundry day, and the cook could put on a pot of beans to simmer for hours while she washed the clothes. If we had our way, every cook in New Orleans would have a pressure cooker to make this great meal anytime without setting aside half a day to do it!

    2 tablespoons olive oil
    1 pound andouille or other smoked sausage,
        cut into ½-inch-thick rounds
    1 large onion, chopped
    2 medium celery ribs with leaves, chopped
    1 medium red bell pepper, seeded and chopped
    2 garlic cloves, minced
    1 tablespoon Cajun Seasoning (page 66)
    1 pound dried small red beans, soaked and drained
        (see page 72)
    3 cups Homemade Beef Stock (page 14) or
        canned low-sodium broth
    Salt, to taste
    6 cups hot cooked rice (2 cups raw rice)

1. In a 5- to 7-quart pressure cooker, heat 1 tablespoon of the oil over medium-high heat. Add the sausage and cook, turning occasionally, until lightly browned, about 5 minutes. Add the onion, celery, red pepper, and garlic. Cook, stirring often, until the vegetables begin to soften, about 3 minutes. Stir in the Cajun Seasoning. Add the beans and stock. If necessary, add enough water to the cooker to cover the beans. Drizzle the remaining 1 tablespoon oil on top.

2. Lock the lid in place. Bring to high pressure over high heat. Adjust the heat to maintain the pressure. Cook for 7 minutes. Remove from the heat and quick-release the pressure. Open the lid, tilting it away from you to block any escaping steam.

3. Return the cooker to medium heat and bring to a simmer. Cook until the beans are tender, mashing some beans into the broth to thicken as desired, about 5 minutes. Season with salt.

4. To serve, ladle the beans into soup bowls and top with a spoonful of rice.

Makes 8 servings
7 minutes at high pressure

BEANS

82

risotto
and grains

When pressure cooking began its resurgence a few years ago, pressure-cooked risotto was the big surprise. Everyone expected the pressure cooker to turn out great stew, but risotto…? The delicate darling of Italian restaurants? The famous rice dish that requires constant stirring and attention, banishing the home cook to the kitchen to slave away while ignoring the guests in the living room?

Yes, you can make terrific risotto in 6 minutes in the pressure cooker. The steam and pressure combine to make a no-stir risotto that isn't just passable, it's *great!* With these recipes and a pressure cooker, risotto is likely to become a standard meal at your house.

The pressure cooker does a fine job with other grains, too. We've concentrated on the ones that we think you'll cook most often. We save the pressure cooker to prepare long-cooking grains like brown rice and wild rice. For plain white rice, most manufacturers recommend low pressure, and many models come with only a high setting. Besides, long-grain rice takes only 15 minutes to cook. We would rather have our pressure cooker free for making the main course and prepare the rice in a traditional saucepan. However, we do make a one-pot meal, Spanish Rice with Sausage (page 89), with long-grain rice in the pressure cooker.

tips for **risotto**

➤ To make risotto, you must use a medium-grain rice. This rice contains sufficient starch to give risotto its creamy texture. The most popular rice for risotto is Arborio, from Italy (there is also a California-grown Arborio); however, it is popular mainly because it is relatively easy to grow and has flooded the market. If you can find them, Carnaroli and Vialone Nano varieties have superior texture and flavor, and while somewhat expensive, they are worth the extra money.

➤ The exact cooking time varies with different brands of rice. When you find a brand you like, stick with it. If the risotto needs more cooking (it should be al dente, but not hard), stir in about ½ cup of broth and simmer uncovered over medium-low heat, stirring almost constantly, until the rice is the desired texture and the cooking liquid has a loose, creamy consistency.

➤ The risotto recipes can be halved to make fewer servings. You do not have to use a different-sized pot.

➤ A 2½-quart skillet-shaped cooker is the ideal utensil for pressure-cooked risotto. If you love risotto, you'll want to have one of these cookers. However, any 5- to 7-quart cooker will do the job.

➤ If you wish, stir an additional 2 tablespoons of butter into the risotto just before serving. It adds an exquisite richness, though it is an indulgence.

risotto with **porcini** and **parmesan**

Arlene makes this risotto all the time for a quick supper. She believes that every kitchen should be stocked with basic staples that allow a cook to make impromptu meals. She is never without the Italian rice, dried mushrooms, canned broth, or Parmesan cheese to make this satisfying dish. (And if you have some gorgonzola or other blue cheese on hand, toss that in, too.)

1 ounce (1 cup) dried porcini mushrooms
4 tablespoons unsalted butter
1 medium onion, chopped
2 garlic cloves, minced
1½ cups rice for risotto (Arborio, Carnaroli, or Vialone Nano)
½ cup dry white wine
2 cups boiling water
1½ cups Homemade Chicken Stock (page 13) or canned low-sodium broth, plus more as needed
½ cup freshly grated Parmesan cheese
½ cup crumbled Gorgonzola cheese (optional)
Salt and freshly ground black pepper, to taste

1. Rinse the dried mushrooms under cold running water to remove any grit. Chop coarsely and set aside.

2. In a 5- to 7-quart pressure cooker, melt 2 tablespoons of the butter over medium heat. Add the onion and cook until softened, about 3 minutes. Stir in the reserved mushrooms and the garlic and cook for 30 seconds. Add the rice and stir constantly until the rice is well-coated with butter but not browned, about 1 minute. Add the wine and cook until it is almost completely evaporated, about 2 minutes. Add the water and broth.

3. Lock the lid in place. Bring to high pressure over high heat. Adjust the heat to maintain pressure. Cook for 6 minutes. Remove from the heat and quick-release the pressure. Open the lid, tilting it away from you to block any escaping steam. Taste the risotto; it should be barely tender (al dente). If necessary, return to medium-low heat, add ½ cup broth or water, and stir until the rice is tender and the liquid is creamy. Stir in the Parmesan cheese, and Gorgonzola if desired. Stir in the remaining 2 tablespoons butter. Season with salt and pepper. Serve immediately.

Risotto with Two Mushrooms: In a large skillet, heat 2 tablespoons unsalted butter over medium heat. Add one large portobello mushroom, chopped into ½-inch cubes. Cook until the mushroom is tender, about 6 minutes. Season with salt and pepper. Stir the cooked portobello mushroom into the risotto just before serving.

Makes 4 main-course or 6 to 8 first-course servings
6 minutes at high pressure

shrimp and saffron risotto

The shrimp for this elegant and easy risotto are cut lengthwise into two thin halves. This allows them to be better distributed throughout the dish. However, take care not to overcook them, because after their initial sauté, they will be reheated in the hot risotto. In some parts of Italy where cheese is scarce but fish is abundant, cooks warn against serving cheese with fish or shellfish. This dictum evolved for agricultural and geographical reasons rather than culinary good sense (as cheese and fish can be delicious together), so add the Parmesan, if you wish.

4 tablespoons unsalted butter
1 pound medium shrimp, peeled (save shells for stock, if desired), deveined, and cut in halves lengthwise
¼ teaspoon crumbled saffron threads
½ cup dry white wine
1 medium onion, chopped
2 garlic cloves, minced
1½ cups rice for risotto (Arborio, Carnaroli, or Vialone Nano)
3½ cups Shrimp Stock (recipe follows), or 1½ cups canned low-sodium chicken broth, 1 cup bottled clam juice, and 1 cup water, plus more broth or water as needed
½ teaspoon salt, plus more to taste
¼ teaspoon freshly ground black pepper, plus more to taste
1 large ripe tomato, seeded and cut into ½-inch cubes
2 tablespoons chopped fresh parsley
Freshly grated Parmesan cheese, for serving

1. In a 5- to 7-quart pressure cooker, melt 2 tablespoons of the butter over medium heat. Add the shrimp and cook just until they turn pink, about 2 minutes. Using a slotted spoon, transfer the shrimp to a plate and set aside.

2. Stir the saffron into the wine and set aside. Add the remaining 2 tablespoons butter to the pot and heat over medium heat. Add the onion and garlic and cook just until beginning to soften, about 1 minute. Add the rice and stir constantly until it is well coated with butter but not browned, about 1 minute. Add the saffron-wine and cook until it is almost completely evaporated, about 2 minutes. Stir in the shrimp stock and season with ½ teaspoon salt and ¼ teaspoon pepper.

3. Lock the lid in place. Bring to high pressure over high heat. Adjust the heat to maintain pressure. Cook for 6 minutes. Remove from the heat and quick-release the pressure. Open the lid, tilting it away from you to block any escaping steam. Taste the risotto; it should be barely tender (al dente). If necessary, return to medium-low heat, add ½ cup water, and stir until the rice is tender. Just before serving, stir in the shrimp, tomato, and parsley. Season with additional salt and pepper. Serve immediately, with the cheese passed on the side.

Shrimp Stock: In a 5- to 7-quart pressure cooker, combine the shells from 1 pound shrimp, 3 cups water, 1 cup bottled clam juice or canned low-sodium chicken broth, 1 small onion and 1 small celery rib with leaves (both chopped), 4 parsley sprigs, ¼ teaspoon dried thyme, and ¼ teaspoon whole black peppercorns. Lock the lid in place. Bring to high pressure over high heat. Adjust the heat to maintain the pressure. Cook for 5 minutes. Quick-release the pressure. Strain the stock into a medium bowl. Yield: About 3½ cups.

———

Makes 4 main-course or 6 to 8 first-course servings
6 minutes at high pressure

spanish rice with **sausage**

When Arlene's kids were growing up, this was one of their favorite meals, and she always made it in the pressure cooker. It is still popular with the kids in our families. If you wish, stir ½ cup thawed petite peas and a couple of tablespoons chopped fresh basil into the rice just before serving.

2 tablespoons olive oil
1 medium onion, chopped
2 medium celery ribs, chopped
1 garlic clove, finely chopped
1 pound sweet Italian pork or turkey sausage, casings removed
1½ cups long-grain rice
¼ teaspoon dried oregano
¼ teaspoon salt
¼ teaspoon freshly ground black pepper
2½ cups Homemade Chicken Stock (page 13) or canned low-sodium broth
One 14½-ounce can tomatoes in juice, drained and chopped, juices reserved

1. In a 5- to 7-quart pressure cooker, heat the oil over medium-high heat. Add the onion, celery, and garlic. Cook, stirring often, until the vegetables begin to soften, about 2 minutes. Add the sausage and cook, breaking it up with the side of a spoon, until it loses its raw look, about 7 minutes. Pour off any excess fat from the cooker.

2. Add the rice, oregano, salt, and pepper and stir well. Add the stock and the tomatoes and their juice.

3. Lock the lid in place. Bring to high pressure over high heat. Adjust the heat to maintain the pressure. Cook for 6 minutes. Remove from the heat and quick-release the pressure. Open the lid, tilting it away from you to block any escaping steam. Stir well. Serve immediately.

___

Makes 6 main-course servings
6 minutes at high pressure

risotto with butternut squash and sausage

This satisfying risotto may be too rich for a first course unless the entrée is something quite light (we like to serve it as an opener to grilled fish).

1 pound (½ medium) butternut squash, peeled, seeded, and cut into 1-inch cubes

4 tablespoons unsalted butter

1 pound sweet Italian pork sausage, casings removed

1 medium onion, chopped

1½ cups rice for risotto (Arborio, Carnaroli, or Vialone Nano)

½ cup dry white wine

3½ cups Homemade Chicken Stock (page 13) or canned low-sodium broth, plus more as needed

¼ teaspoon salt, plus more to taste

¼ teaspoon freshly ground black pepper, plus more to taste

½ cup freshly grated Parmesan cheese

A few gratings of fresh nutmeg

Chopped fresh sage, for garnish

1. Place the trivet and steaming basket in a 5- to 7-quart pressure cooker. Add 2 cups water to the cooker. Place the squash in the basket. Lock the lid in place. Bring to high pressure over high heat. Cook for 1½ minutes. Remove from the heat and quick-release the pressure. Open the lid, tilting it away from you to block any escaping steam. Remove the squash from the cooker and set aside.

2. Rinse and dry the cooker. Add 2 tablespoons of the butter to the cooker and melt over medium heat. Add the sausage and onion and cook, stirring often and breaking up the sausage with a spoon, until the sausage loses its raw look, about 6 minutes. Do not brown the sausage. Pour off all but 2 tablespoons of the fat. Add the rice and cook, stirring often, until well-coated, about 2 minutes. Add the wine and bring to a boil. Stir in the stock, ¼ teaspoon salt, and ¼ teaspoon pepper.

3. Lock the lid in place. Bring to high pressure over high heat. Adjust the heat to maintain pressure. Cook for 6 minutes. Remove from the heat and quick-release the pressure. Open the lid, tilting it away from you to block any escaping steam. Taste the risotto; it should be barely tender (al dente). If necessary, return to medium-low heat, add ½ cup stock or water, and stir until the rice is tender and the liquid is creamy. Stir in the reserved squash, Parmesan cheese, and the remaining 2 tablespoons butter. Season with the nutmeg and additional salt and pepper. Serve immediately, garnishing each serving with the sage.

Makes 4 main-course or 6 to 8 first-course servings
1½ minutes at high pressure for the squash, then
6 minutes at high pressure for the risotto

polenta with **gorgonzola**

If you have a pressure cooker with a nonstick lining, you'll never have to stir a pot of polenta again. (Unfortunately, polenta sticks to regular pots.) For the best texture, use coarse-grain cornmeal or imported Italian polenta. (Don't confuse it with instant polenta.) For a main course, substitute ½ cup freshly grated Parmesan cheese for the gorgonzola, and spoon Wild Mushroom Sauce (page 98) over the polenta.

> 2 cups Homemade Chicken Stock (page 13)
> or canned low-sodium broth
> ¼ teaspoon salt, plus more to taste
> 1 cup coarse-grain cornmeal
> 1 cup water
> 1 tablespoon olive oil
> 3 ounces Gorgonzola or other blue-veined cheese,
> crumbled
> ¼ teaspoon freshly ground black pepper

1. In a nonstick 5- to 7-quart pressure cooker, bring the stock and ¼ teaspoon salt to a boil over high heat. In a medium bowl, whisk the cornmeal and water together, then whisk into the boiling broth. Drizzle the top with the olive oil.

2. Lock the lid in place. Using a heat diffuser, bring to high pressure over high heat. Cook for 2 minutes. Remove from the heat and quick-release the pressure. Open the lid, tilting it away from you to block any escaping steam. Add the gorgonzola and pepper, and stir to melt the cheese. Season with additional salt. Serve immediately.

Makes 4 to 6 side-dish servings
2 minutes at high pressure

quick pasta sauces

You've just rushed in from work, and you're famished. You want something easy to cook, a no-brainer. If you're anything like us, a lot of the time you make a pot of pasta. And it's no compromise, because you love it! It's the pasta sauce that takes some time to pull together, at least if you want that "simmering on the back of the stove for hours like the one Grandma used to make" flavor. (Assuming that Grandma was Italian.)

The bad news is that you gain nothing by cooking pasta in a pressure cooker. (Most manufacturers warn against doing so, and while some intrepid cooks have figured out ways to do it without hurting themselves, we say it's not worth the hassle.) The good news is that you can make *bellissimo* sauces in the pressure cooker in the amount of time it takes for the water to come to a boil and cook the pasta.

The sauces in this chapter call for 1 pound of cooked pasta. If yours is a smaller family, use half of the sauce with 8 ounces of pasta, and freeze the rest for another meal. You'll have a treasure trove of frozen sauce to thaw in the microwave for the next time you come home from work hassled and hurried.

three-meat **bolognese** sauce

Bolognese sauce, enhanced with a bit of cream, is one of the most glorious concoctions you can put on pasta. This sauce is all about meat—you may notice that it doesn't have the herbs associated with most pasta sauces. We use a meat-loaf mixture (equal parts of beef, veal, and pork) to give it a delicate, but rich, flavor. Instead of cooking your sauce for hours, pressure-cook it for 15 minutes, and take pride in the speedy but tasty result. It is particularly luscious with fresh fettucine.

1 tablespoon unsalted butter
1 medium onion, chopped
1 medium carrot, chopped
1 medium celery rib with leaves, chopped
1 garlic clove, minced
1½ pounds meat-loaf mixture, or 8 ounces each ground round, ground pork, and ground veal
½ cup dry white wine, such as Pinot Grigio or Sauvignon Blanc
One 14½-ounce can tomatoes in juice, drained and chopped, juices reserved
2 tablespoons tomato paste
1 bay leaf
½ teaspoon salt
¼ teaspoon freshly ground black pepper
½ cup heavy cream

1. In a 5- to 7-quart pressure cooker, melt the butter over medium-high heat. Add the onion, carrot, celery, and garlic. Cook, stirring occasionally, until the vegetables begin to soften, about 2 minutes. Add the meat-loaf mixture and cook, breaking up the meat with a spoon, until the meat loses its pink color, about 5 minutes. Pour off the excess fat from the pot. (If desired, drain the meat and vegetables in a wire sieve, and return the solids to the pot.)

2. Add the wine and boil until reduced by about half, about 2 minutes. Stir in the chopped tomatoes and their juice, tomato paste, bay leaf, salt, and pepper. Lock the lid in place. Bring to high pressure over high heat. Adjust the heat to maintain the pressure. Cook for 15 minutes.

3. Remove from the heat and quick-release the pressure. Open the lid, tilting it away from you to block any escaping steam. Return the uncovered pot to medium-high heat and bring the sauce to a boil. Add the cream and cook until the sauce is slightly thickened, about 5 minutes.

Makes about 4 cups sauce
15 minutes at high pressure

summer tomato and **basil** sauce

Plum tomatoes make the best tomato sauce. (Large beefsteak tomatoes are great sliced in salads, but are too juicy for the saucepot.) The seeds must be removed or the sauce will be too thin, yet the skins are kept on to give the sauce body. You'll need only ¼ cup water to get the sauce to come up to pressure, as the tomatoes give off juice as they cook. (In fact, you may not need any water at all. Try to bring the sauce up to pressure without the water, and add the water only if pressure isn't reached.) Instead of Parmesan cheese, drizzle each serving of pasta with a little extra olive oil.

to a food processor fitted with the metal blade and purée. Add the basil and pulse to combine. Season with the salt.

———

Makes about 4 cups sauce
6 minutes at high pressure

1 tablespoon extra-virgin olive oil
2 garlic cloves
4 pounds ripe plum tomatoes, cut in half
   lengthwise and squeezed gently to remove seeds
¼ cup water, optional (see above)
¼ teaspoon crushed hot red pepper flakes
½ cup chopped fresh basil
½ teaspoon salt

1. In a 5- to 7-quart pressure cooker, heat the oil over medium heat. Add the garlic and cook, stirring often, until softened, about 1 minute. Stir in the tomatoes, water, if desired, and hot pepper.

2. Lock the lid in place. Bring to high pressure over high heat. Adjust the heat to maintain the pressure. Cook for 6 minutes. Remove from the heat and quick-release the pressure. Open the lid, tilting it away from you to block any escaping steam.

3. Return the cooker to medium heat. Boil the sauce, uncovered, stirring often until slightly thickened, about 5 minutes. Transfer the tomato mixture

sicilian tomato and **pork** sauce

This is a light-bodied meat-infused sauce that clings well to pasta—try it with ziti or rigatoni. The secret ingredient is pork neck bones, which are available at most supermarkets (at least the ones that cater to smart ethnic cooks who know that pork neck bones pack a lot of flavor for very little money). Serve the pasta with plenty of freshly grated Parmesan or Romano cheese.

3 tablespoons olive oil
2 pounds pork neck bones, sawed into large pieces
1 large onion, chopped
2 garlic cloves, minced
1 teaspoon dried oregano
1 teaspoon dried basil
1/8 teaspoon crushed hot red pepper flakes
1 bay leaf
1/2 cup hearty red wine, such as Zinfandel
One 28-ounce can crushed tomatoes
Salt, to taste

1. In a 5- to 7-quart pressure cooker, heat 2 tablespoons of the oil over medium-high heat. In batches, add the neck bones and cook until browned on both sides, about 4 minutes. Transfer to a plate and set aside.

2. Add the remaining 1 tablespoon oil to the pot and heat. Add the onion and garlic and cook until softened, about 2 minutes. Stir in the oregano, basil, crushed red pepper, and bay leaf. Add the wine and boil until reduced by half, about 2 minutes. Stir in the tomatoes. Return the pork bones to the pot.

3. Lock the lid in place. Bring to high pressure over high heat. Adjust the heat to maintain the pressure. Cook for 40 minutes. Remove from the heat and quick-release the pressure. Open the lid, tilting it away from you to block any escaping steam.

4. Transfer the bones to a cutting board. Using a fork, pull the meat from the bones (don't worry about getting every last morsel—just the substantial pieces are enough) and discard the bones. Shred the meat and return to the sauce. Season the sauce with salt.

Sicilian Tomato and Ricotta Pasta: Toss the sauce with one pound cooked pasta and one 15-ounce container ricotta cheese, at room temperature. (Chilled ricotta will cool the pasta too much.)

Makes about 4 cups sauce
40 minutes at high pressure

wild mushroom sauce

Here's a quick pasta sauce with deep, earthy flavors. It's best on sturdy pasta, like ziti or rigatoni. Dried mushrooms are usually soaked for 20 minutes or so to soften before cooking, but that step is unnecessary with a pressure cooker.

quick-release the pressure. Open the lid, tilting it away from you to block any escaping steam. Stir in the parsley.

Makes about 3½ cups sauce
5 minutes at high pressure

1 cup (1 ounce) dried porcini mushrooms
2 tablespoons olive oil
1 medium onion, chopped
2 garlic cloves, finely chopped
1 pound fresh white mushrooms, sliced
1 cup boiling Homemade Chicken Stock (page 13) or canned low-sodium broth
One 14½-ounce can tomatoes in juice, drained and chopped
2 tablespoons tomato paste
¼ teaspoon dried rosemary
¼ teaspoon dried sage
¼ teaspoon salt
¼ teaspoon freshly ground black pepper
2 tablespoons chopped fresh parsley

1. Rinse the dried mushrooms under cold running water to remove the grit. Chop coarsely and set aside.

2. In a 5- to 7-quart pressure cooker, heat the oil over medium heat. Add the onion and garlic and cook, stirring often, until the vegetables begin to soften, about 2 minutes. Add the fresh mushrooms and cook, stirring often, until softened, about 5 minutes. Stir in the broth, the tomatoes, tomato paste, rosemary, sage, salt, and pepper.

3. Lock the lid in place. Bring to high pressure over high heat. Adjust the heat to maintain the pressure. Cook for 5 minutes. Remove from the heat and

spaghetti and meatballs

It's pretty safe to say that everyone loves spaghetti and meatballs, especially kids. This pressure-cooked version brings this crowd-pleaser on the table in under 30 minutes, from start to finish (depending on how long it takes for the pasta water to come to a boil). There is only one way to mix the meatball mixture: use your hands, well-washed before and after mixing, of course.

SAUCE
- 1 tablespoon olive oil
- 1 medium onion, chopped
- 2 garlic cloves, finely chopped
- One 28-ounce can crushed tomatoes
- ½ teaspoon dried basil
- ½ teaspoon dried oregano
- ¼ teaspoon crushed hot red pepper flakes

MEATBALLS
- ½ cup fresh Italian or French bread crumbs (make in a blender or food processor)
- ¼ cup milk
- 1½ pounds meat loaf mixture, or 8 ounces each ground round, ground pork, and ground veal
- 1 small onion, finely chopped
- 1 garlic clove, finely chopped
- 1 large egg, beaten
- ½ teaspoon dried basil
- ½ teaspoon salt
- ⅛ teaspoon freshly ground black pepper

- 1 pound spaghetti, cooked
- Freshly grated Parmesan cheese, for serving

1. To make the sauce: In a 5- to 7-quart pressure cooker, heat the oil over medium-high heat. Add the onion and garlic. Cook, stirring often, until the onion begins to soften, about 2 minutes. Stir in the tomatoes, basil, oregano, and hot pepper.

2. Bring to high pressure over high heat. Adjust the heat to maintain the pressure. Cook for 15 minutes. Remove from the heat and quick-release the pressure. Open the lid, tilting it away from you to block any escaping steam. Return the uncovered pot to medium-high heat and bring the sauce to a boil.

3. Meanwhile, prepare the meatballs: In a medium bowl, mix the bread crumbs and milk; let stand 5 minutes. Add the meat-loaf mixture, onion, garlic, egg, basil, salt, and pepper. Using your hands, mix thoroughly. Using about 2 tablespoons for each meatball, form into 2-inch balls.

4. One at a time, place the meatballs in the simmering sauce, shaking the pan as needed to get the meatballs to fit (as much as possible) in one layer. Lock the lid in place. Bring to high pressure over high heat. Adjust the heat to maintain the pressure and cook for 5 minutes. Remove from the heat and quick-release the pressure. Open the lid, tilting it away from you to block any escaping steam.

5. Using a slotted spoon, transfer the meatballs to a plate. In a large bowl, toss the spaghetti with the sauce, then top with the meatballs. Serve immediately, with the cheese passed on the side.

Makes 6 servings
15 minutes at high pressure for sauce,
then 5 minutes at high pressure for meatballs

broccoli rabe and sausage sauce

QUICK PASTA SAUCES

Broccoli rabe, also called rapini, used to be found only in Italian-neighborhood grocers. Now it has gone mainstream, although in some areas you will find it only during the winter months. With its long, thin stems and leafy florets, broccoli rabe looks like regular broccoli in need of a barber. It has a bracing, slightly bitter flavor that is best tempered with sausage and plenty of garlic. The pressure cooker makes short work out of the traditionally lengthy cooking time. This sauce doesn't freeze well, so toss it right after cooking with hot ziti or rigatoni, and offer Parmesan cheese on the side.

2 tablespoons olive oil
1 pound sweet Italian pork sausage, casings removed
2 garlic cloves, chopped
2 pounds broccoli rabe
1 cup Homemade Chicken Stock (page 13) or canned low-sodium broth
¼ teaspoon crushed hot red pepper
Salt, to taste

1. In a 5- to 7-quart pressure cooker, heat the oil over medium heat. Add the sausage and cook, breaking up with the side of a spoon, until the sausage loses its pink look, about 5 minutes. Add the garlic and cook for 1 minute.

2. While the sausage is cooking, rinse the broccoli rabe well. Shake off excess water but do not dry completely. Cut the stems into ½-inch-long pieces, and coarsely chop the florets. Set aside.

3. In 3 or 4 batches, stir in the broccoli rabe, letting the first batch wilt somewhat before adding another. Pour in the stock and add the crushed red pepper. Lock the lid in place. Bring to high pressure over high heat. Adjust the heat to maintain the pressure. Cook for 5 minutes. Remove from the heat and quick-release the steam. Open the lid, tilting it away from you to block any escaping steam. Season with the salt.

___

Makes 4 to 6 servings
5 minutes at high pressure

vegetables

When gathering vegetable dishes for this book, we decided to stick to the ones that required long cooking and would benefit from pressure cooking. In our experience, cooking times for the more delicate vegetables vary from cooker to cooker, and it is best to follow the instructions in your cooker's manual. Besides, you probably don't need a "recipe" for steamed carrots tossed with butter. (We do provide instructions for some simple potato dishes, because there are specific ways to prepare them to ensure success.) Also, these days, the cooked texture of many favorite vegetables (broccoli, carrots, and others) is a matter of taste. Some like them crisp-tender, and others well done. It is easier to gauge doneness in a traditional pot. The vegetables we've included here are all at their best when cooked until tender, so there's a minimum of guesswork.

tips for vegetables

➤ Use fresh, flavorful vegetables. Any off-flavors will be intensified in the cooker.

➤ When cooking potatoes, cut them into uniform pieces. Whole potatoes, even small new potatoes, tend to crack and cook unevenly in the pressure cooker.

artichokes with minted vegetable broth

If you have been disappointed by bland pressure-cooked artichokes, as we have, this recipe is for you. The problem is solved by pressure-cooking the artichokes over a delicious broth, which adds much-needed flavor. The broth is served with the artichokes as a dipping sauce, and is so tasty you'll want to serve it with crusty bread. It is important to use medium-sized artichokes, as large ones rarely seem to be cooked through to the heart even though the leaves are tender.

Four medium (8 ounces each) artichokes
1 lemon, halved crosswise
1 tablespoon extra-virgin olive oil, plus more for
    serving
1 medium onion, chopped
1 medium carrot, chopped
1 medium celery rib with leaves, chopped
2 garlic cloves, minced
1 cup Homemade Chicken Stock (page 13) or
    canned low-sodium broth
¼ teaspoon salt
2 tablespoons chopped fresh mint
Crusty Italian bread, for serving

1. Using a heavy knife, cut off the stems and top inch from each artichoke. If desired, using kitchen shears, snip the prickly tips from the leaves. Rub the cut surfaces with the lemon. Set aside.

2. In a 5- to 7-quart pressure cooker, heat 1 table-spoon of the oil over medium heat. Add the onion, carrot, celery, and garlic. Cook, stirring often, until the vegetables begin to soften, about 2 minutes. Add the stock and salt and bring to a boil. Place the trivet and steamer basket in the cooker. Stack the artichokes in the basket, pyramid-style.

3. Lock the lid in place. Bring to high pressure over high heat. Adjust the heat to maintain the pressure. Cook for 15 minutes. Remove from the heat and quick-release the pressure. Open the lid, tilting it away from you to block any escaping steam.

4. Using kitchen tongs, place each artichoke in a deep soup bowl. Stir the mint into the broth. Ladle the broth around the artichokes. Serve hot, with the bread passed on the side to sop up the juices, and a cruet of oil for drizzling.

Makes 4 servings
15 minutes at high pressure

german **red cabbage** with bacon and apples

Of course, in the old days, almost every kitchen had a pot of rendered bacon fat (gathered from the daily fried breakfast bacon) in the refrigerator. Now, we cook a few strips of bacon for the recipe to lend its smoky, meaty flavor to the cabbage. Serve this classic with grilled pork chops (smoked chops are especially good). The red wine and vinegar are essential to keep the cabbage from losing its color.

1 tablespoon vegetable oil
3 bacon strips, coarsely chopped
1 medium onion, chopped
2 Granny Smith apples, peeled, seeded, and cut lengthwise into quarters
½ cup fruity red wine, such as Merlot
⅓ cup packed light brown sugar
3 tablespoons red wine vinegar
One medium (2½ pounds) red cabbage, cored and cut into ¼-inch-wide strips
½ teaspoon salt, plus more to taste
¼ teaspoon freshly ground black pepper, plus more to taste

1. In a 5- to 7-quart pressure cooker, heat the oil over medium heat. Add the bacon and cook, stirring occasionally, until crisp and brown, about 5 minutes. Using a slotted spoon, transfer the bacon to paper towels to drain. Pour off all but 2 tablespoons of the fat from the cooker.

2. Return the cooker to medium heat. Add the onion and apples. Cook, uncovered, until the onion begins to soften, about 2 minutes. Stir in the wine, brown sugar, and vinegar and bring to a boil. Gradually stir the cabbage into the cooker, letting each addition wilt before adding another. The cooker should not be more than half-filled. Season with ½ teaspoon salt and ¼ teaspoon pepper.

3. Lock the lid in place. Bring to high pressure over high heat. Adjust the heat to maintain the pressure. Cook for 8 minutes. Remove from the heat and quick-release the pressure. Open the lid, tilting it away from you to block any escaping steam. Season with additional salt and pepper.

4. Using a slotted spoon, transfer the cabbage to a serving dish. Stir in the bacon. Serve hot.

Makes 8 servings
8 minutes at high pressure

V E G E T A B L E S

orange-glazed yams

Sweet candied yams are a holiday menu staple. They can be stubborn and often take quite awhile to cook through, but not when a pressure cooker is around. Because they're rich, three yams will probably suffice for six to eight servings. Use orange-fleshed Louisiana yams, not pale yellow sweet potatoes (they're actually quite different, and the Louisiana yams are much sweeter). It's important to choose long, narrow yams, which will cook more evenly than large, round ones.

½ cup fresh orange juice

½ cup water (or more to meet your cooker's minimum liquid requirement)

3 medium (10 ounces each) Louisiana yams, preferably with long, narrow shapes, peeled and cut lengthwise

⅓ cup packed light brown sugar

Grated zest of ½ orange

⅛ teaspoon salt

2 tablespoons unsalted butter, in small pieces

1. Pour the orange juice and water into a 5- to 7-quart pressure cooker. Fit with the steamer basket. Stack the yams in the basket, sprinkling with the brown sugar, orange zest, and salt, and dotting with the butter.

2. Lock the lid in place. Bring to high pressure over high heat. Adjust the heat to maintain the pressure. Cook for 7 minutes. Remove from the heat and quick-release the pressure. Open the lid, tilting it away from you to block any escaping steam. Using the tip of a small sharp knife, check the yams for tenderness. If necessary, cover the pot with the lid (do not lock) and steam the yams over medium heat until tender. Using a slotted spatula or spoon, transfer the yams to a warmed serving dish, and cover with foil to keep warm.

3. Return the uncovered pot to high heat and bring the cooking liquid to a boil. Boil until thickened, 3 to 5 minutes (about 10 minutes if more than ½ cup water was used). Using a small knife, cut the yams into chunks. Pour the glaze over the yams and serve hot.

Makes 6 to 8 servings

7 minutes at high pressure

scalloped **cauliflower** and mushrooms

Cauliflower in cheese sauce may sound like a somewhat common dish, but this version gets a lift from leeks and dried porcini mushrooms. It's made in the pressure cooker, then run under the broiler to give it a nice finish. Serve alongside grilled fish fillets, or as a vegetarian main course.

3 tablespoons unsalted butter, plus more for the dish

1 cup chopped leeks, white and pale green parts only (3 medium leeks)

½ ounce dried porcini mushrooms, quickly rinsed under cold water and coarsely chopped

1 large (2½ pounds) head cauliflower, trimmed and cut into florets about 1½ inches across

1 cup Homemade Chicken Stock (page 13), canned low-sodium broth, or water

⅛ teaspoon salt, plus more to taste

⅛ teaspoon freshly ground white pepper, plus more to taste

2 tablespoons cornstarch

2 cups half-and-half or milk

1 cup shredded Gruyère or Swiss cheese

2 tablespoons freshly grated Parmesan cheese

1. Position a rack 6 inches from the source of heat and preheat the broiler. Lightly butter a 9 x 13-inch flameproof dish.

2. In a 5- to 7-quart pressure cooker, melt 2 tablespoons butter over medium heat. Add the leeks and dried mushrooms and cook until the leeks soften, about 1 minute. Add the cauliflower, stock, ⅛ teaspoon salt, and ⅛ teaspoon pepper.

3. Lock the lid in place. Bring to high pressure over high heat. Adjust the heat to maintain the pressure. Cook for 30 seconds. Remove from the heat and quick-release the pressure. Open the lid, tilting it away from you to block any escaping steam. Using a slotted spoon, transfer the cauliflower to the prepared dish. Cover with foil to keep warm and set aside. Return the uncovered pot to medium heat and bring to a boil.

4. In a small bowl, sprinkle the cornstarch over the half-and-half and whisk until dissolved. Whisk into the pot and cook until thickened. Remove from the heat and stir in the Gruyère cheese until smooth. Season with additional salt and pepper. Pour over the cauliflower. Sprinkle with the Parmesan cheese and dot with the remaining 1 tablespoon butter.

5. Broil until the top is lightly browned, 1 to 2 minutes. Serve hot.

Makes 6 to 8 servings
30 seconds at high pressure

steamed potatoes with dill butter

Steamed potatoes have a lovely simplicity that makes them a favorite side dish. To make them in a pressure cooker, slice them first—whole potatoes have a tendency to split. Medium-sized potatoes cook more evenly than large ones.

2½ pounds medium red-skinned potatoes, peeled and cut into ¼-inch-thick rounds
Salt, to taste
3 tablespoons unsalted butter
2 tablespoons chopped fresh dill
Freshly ground black pepper, to taste

1. Place a collapsible aluminum steamer in a 5- to 7-quart pressure cooker (the steamer holds more potatoes than the typical steamer basket that comes with most cookers). Add the minimum amount of water as required by your cooker to bring up to pressure. This could be anywhere from ½ cup to 1½ cups, but do not let the water touch the bottom of the steamer. Place the potatoes in the steamer, seasoning them lightly with salt. Lock the lid in place. Bring to high pressure over high heat. Adjust the heat to maintain pressure. Cook for 2 minutes, 45 seconds. Remove from the heat and quick-release the pressure. Open the lid, tilting it away from you to block any escaping steam. Using the tip of a small sharp knife, check the potatoes for tenderness. If necessary, cover the pot with the lid (do not lock) and steam the potatoes over medium heat until tender.

2. Transfer the potatoes to a medium bowl. Add the butter and dill and toss. Season with pepper and salt. Serve immediately.

Makes 4 to 6 servings
2 minutes, 45 seconds at high pressure

quick garlic mashed potatoes

Mashed potatoes in less than 15 minutes from start to finish?!

3 pounds medium Idaho or russet potatoes, peeled and cut into ½-inch slices

4 cups water

8 large garlic cloves, crushed under a knife and peeled

½ teaspoon salt, plus more to taste

½ cup hot milk

3 tablespoons unsalted butter

¼ teaspoon freshly ground black pepper

1. In a 5- to 7-quart pressure cooker, combine the potatoes, water, garlic, and ½ teaspoon salt. Lock the lid in place. Bring to high pressure over high heat. Cook for 5 minutes. Remove from the heat and quick-release the pressure. Open the lid, tilting it away from you to block any escaping steam. Drain well.

2. Return the potatoes and garlic to the warm cooker. Using an electric hand mixer or a potato masher, mash the potatoes with the milk and butter. Season with additional salt and the pepper. Serve hot.

Makes 4 servings
5 minutes at high pressure

potato salad with mustard and herbs

Here's Arlene's potato salad *à la française,* with bright and fresh flavors. It's a good choice for a warm summer salad because it won't spoil as quickly as mayonnaise-based versions. There are a few tricks to getting the potatoes cooked into firm, yet tender, slices. Use a collapsible aluminum steamer to hold the potatoes in the pot so they aren't submerged in water. Be sure to use waxy-fleshed red or white potatoes—they will hold their shape better than starchy russets or Idaho potatoes. And don't cut them too thin, or they'll fall apart. It is better to err on the thick side and have to steam undercooked slices for a few extra minutes than have mushy, crumbled potatoes.

2½ pounds medium red-skinned potatoes, peeled and cut into ¼-inch-thick rounds
3 tablespoons dry white wine or dry vermouth
½ teaspoon salt, plus more to taste
2 tablespoons white wine vinegar
1 tablespoon Dijon mustard
⅓ cup olive oil
1 tablespoon finely chopped fresh rosemary
1 tablespoon finely chopped fresh chives
Freshly ground black pepper, to taste

1. Place a collapsible aluminum steamer in a 5- to 7-quart pressure cooker (the steamer holds more potatoes than the typical steamer basket that comes with most cookers). Add the minimum amount of water as required by your cooker to bring up to pressure. This could be anywhere from ½ cup to 1½ cups, but do not let the water touch the bottom of the steamer. Place the potatoes in the steamer. Lock the lid in place. Bring to high pressure over high heat. Adjust the heat to maintain pressure. Cook for 2 minutes, 45 seconds. Remove from the heat and quick-release the pressure. Open the lid, tilting it away from you to block any escaping steam. Using the tip of a small sharp knife, check the potatoes for tenderness. If necessary, cover the pot with the lid (do not lock) and steam the potatoes over medium heat until tender.

2. Transfer the potatoes to a medium bowl. Toss with the wine and ½ teaspoon salt, taking care not to break up the slices too much. In a small bowl, whisk together the vinegar and mustard. Gradually whisk in the oil. Stir in the rosemary and chives. Fold into the potatoes. Season with pepper and additional salt. Serve warm or cooled to room temperature, but not chilled.

Makes 4 to 6 servings
2 minutes, 45 seconds at high pressure

moroccan vegetable **stew** with sweet spices and raisins

Moroccan cooks love the interplay of sweet flavors with savory ones. The natural sweetness of butternut squash, carrots, and raisins is tempered by the spices and lemon juice. Spoon the stew over couscous or rice.

2 tablespoons olive oil

1 medium onion, chopped

2 medium carrots, cut into ½-inch-thick rounds

2 garlic cloves, minced

½ teaspoon paprika, preferably sweet Hungarian

½ teaspoon ground cumin

¼ teaspoon ground cinnamon

¼ teaspoon salt

⅛ teaspoon ground hot red pepper flakes

One small (1¾ pounds) butternut squash, peeled, seeded, and cut into 1-inch pieces

One 14½-ounce can tomatoes in juice, drained and chopped

½ cup Homemade Vegetable Stock (page 16), canned vegetable broth, or low-sodium chicken broth

½ cup raisins

2 tablespoons fresh lemon juice

1 teaspoon sugar

Hot cooked couscous, for serving

1. In a 5- to 7-quart pressure cooker, heat the oil over medium-high heat. Add the onion, carrots, and garlic. Cook, stirring often, until the vegetables soften, about 2 minutes. Add the paprika, cumin, cinnamon, salt, and hot pepper and stir until fragrant, about 20 seconds. Stir in the squash, tomatoes, and stock.

2. Lock the lid in place. Bring to high pressure over high heat. Adjust the heat to maintain the pressure. Cook for 3 minutes. Remove from the heat and quick-release the pressure. Open the lid, tilting it away from you to block any escaping steam. Stir in the raisins, lemon juice, and sugar. Let stand for 2 minutes.

3. Serve hot, spooned over the couscous.

Makes 4 to 6 servings
3 minutes at high pressure

desserts and fruits

What a pleasure it is to serve a wonderful dessert in the middle of the summer without having to turn on the oven! Pressure-cooked cheesecakes are so moist and creamy, we rarely make them in the oven anymore. Custards from the pressure cooker turn out so silky-smooth that our pastry chef friends ask for our secret recipe. We love telling them that it's not a secret recipe, but a "secret" cooking appliance. With the pressure cooker, you can prepare elegant, light fruit desserts like Riesling-poached pears and dried fruit compote in a few minutes.

Some pressure-cooked desserts use special pans or containers, which you may already have in your kitchen. You'll need a 7-inch springform pan for cheesecakes, a 1½-quart soufflé dish for bread puddings, and 4- to 5-ounce custard cups or ramekins for custards. All are easily available at kitchenware stores and by mail order from Adventures in Cooking, Wayne, NJ (adventuresincooking.com).

Getting a springform pan or soufflé dish in and out of a pressure cooker may seem awkward, but an aluminum foil "cradle" makes it easy: Tear off a 24-inch length of aluminum foil. Fold the strip lengthwise in half, then in half again, to make a sturdy strip of foil about 3 inches wide. Place the strip on a work surface. Place the pan or soufflé dish in the center of the strip, and bring up the ends. Using the ends as a handle, the dessert can be lifted in and out of the pot. Fold the foil handles down over the dessert when closing the cooker.

tips for **desserts**

➤ When covering cooking containers for pressure cooking, use heavy-duty aluminum foil—it keeps out moisture better than regular foil.

➤ If you plan to do a lot of dessert-making in your cooker, store the foil strip with the pot to use again.

➤ Sometimes a puddle of water will form on the cheesecake top or custard. Simply lay a piece of paper towel over the water to blot it up.

➤ Bread puddings are best when prepared from firm-textured day-old bread. Let the bread stand at room temperature overnight, uncovered. Or, cut up the bread and bake in a preheated 350°F oven for 10 minutes. Do not toast the bread. The bread will firm as it cools.

➤ Try to serve your bread puddings warm— they're really luscious this way. If you wish, make the bread pudding up to 1 day ahead and refrigerate. When ready to serve, cover with microwave-safe wrap and microwave at medium until warmed through, about 2 minutes.

➤ Why do pressure cookers make such wonderfully smooth custards? Eggs break down into solids and liquids at temperatures above 325°F, and the pressure cooker's internal temperature is only 250°F. Because of the moderate temperature and moist cooking atmosphere, the custards won't get a skin on top, either.

chocolate pots de crème

These elegant, intensely chocolate custards will finish off a meal with a few rich, satisfying bites. Use a high-quality bittersweet chocolate for the best results.

1 cup half-and-half
½ cup plus 2 teaspoons sugar
2 ounces bittersweet chocolate, finely chopped
1 large egg plus 2 large egg yolks
¼ teaspoon vanilla
½ cup heavy cream

1. In a medium saucepan, bring the half-and-half and ½ cup sugar to a simmer over medium heat, stirring often to dissolve the sugar. Remove from the heat and add the chocolate. Let stand 1 minute, then whisk to melt the chocolate.

2. In a medium bowl, whisk the egg, egg yolks, and vanilla to combine. Gradually whisk in the hot cream mixture. Strain through a wire sieve into a large glass measuring cup, and pour evenly into four ½-cup ramekins or custard cups. Cover each ramekin tightly with aluminum foil.

3. Place the trivet and steamer basket in a 5- to 7-quart pressure cooker. Pour 2 cups water into the cooker. Stack the cups, pyramid-style, in the cooker. Lock the lid in place. Bring to high pressure over high heat. Adjust the heat to maintain the pressure. Cook for 8 minutes. Remove from the heat and quick-release the pressure. Open the lid, tilting it away from you to block any escaping steam. Let the custards stand in the pot for 3 minutes for easier handling. Using kitchen tongs, remove the cups from the cooker. Remove the foil. The centers should wobble slightly—they will set as they cool. Cool the custards to room temperature. Cover each with plastic wrap and refrigerate until chilled, at least 4 hours.

4. In a chilled small bowl, beat the cream with the remaining 2 teaspoons sugar until thickened. Top each pot de crème with a dollop of whipped cream and serve chilled.

Makes 4 servings
8 minutes at high pressure

orange and **chocolate marble** cheesecake

Serve this cheesecake with fresh strawberries and raspberries for a summertime treat. Use a light dusting of chocolate cookie crumbs, as a thicker crust could overpower the rich filling.

2 tablespoons unsalted butter, melted
¼ cup chocolate wafer or chocolate-flavored graham cracker crumbs
3 ounces bittersweet or semisweet chocolate, finely chopped
1 pound cream cheese, at room temperature
¾ cup sugar
½ cup sour cream
3 tablespoons all-purpose flour
2 teaspoons vanilla extract
Grated zest of 1 orange
3 large eggs plus 1 large egg yolk
Softened butter, for the foil

1. Wrap the bottom of a 7-inch springform pan tightly with heavy-duty aluminum foil. Butter the inside of the pan with all of the melted butter. Sprinkle the bottom of the pan with the cookie crumbs.

2. In the top part of a double boiler over hot, not simmering, water, melt the chocolate, stirring occasionally, until smooth. Remove the top part of the double boiler from the heat and let the chocolate cool until tepid.

3. In a medium bowl, using a hand-held electric mixer set at medium speed, beat the cream cheese and sugar until smooth. Beat in the sour cream, flour, vanilla, and orange zest. Beat in the eggs and egg yolk.

4. Pour about one-fourth of the cheese mixture into the prepared pan. Pour another one-fourth of the mixture into a small bowl and set aside. Stir the cooled chocolate into the remaining cheese mixture until well blended. Pour over the vanilla layer in the pan. Pour the remaining vanilla mixture over the chocolate mixture in a swirl pattern. Run a knife through the two mixtures together to make a marble pattern. Butter a 15-inch-long piece of aluminum foil. Tightly cover the pan with the foil, buttered side down, allowing some room for expansion at the top for the cheesecake to rise. (The foil should completely cover the pan.)

5. Place the trivet in the bottom of a 5- to 7-quart pressure cooker. Pour 2 cups of water into the pot. Center the covered dish in an aluminum foil "cradle" (see page 113). Using the cradle, lower the dish onto the trivet.

6. Lock the lid in place. Bring to high pressure over high heat. Adjust the heat to maintain the pressure. Cook for 25 minutes. Remove from the heat. Allow the pressure to drop naturally, about 20 minutes. Open the lid, tilting it away from you to block any escaping steam.

7. Using the cradle, lift the dish out of the pot. Let stand for 2 or 3 minutes. Remove the foil. If necessary, using paper towels, blot any water on the surface of the cheesecake. Run a sharp knife around the inside of the pan to release the cheesecake from the sides. Place on a wire cake rack and cool completely.

8. Remove the sides of the pan. Cover the cheesecake with plastic wrap and refrigerate until well chilled, at least 4 hours. Serve chilled, using a sharp knife dipped into hot water to cut each slice.

Makes 6 to 8 servings
25 minutes at high pressure

apricot cheesecake

Fresh apricots are a summertime treat, but dried apricots have a more intense flavor that makes them perfect for baking. The filling should be prepared in a food processor to purée the apricots. Otherwise, press the softened apricots through a wire sieve and make the filling with an electric mixer, adding the apricot purée with the eggs.

2 tablespoons unsalted butter, melted
¼ cup crushed amaretti cookies, or use any crisp cookie
8 ounces dried apricots, cut into ¼-inch-wide slices
½ cup water
1 pound cream cheese, at room temperature
¾ cup sugar
¼ cup sour cream, at room temperature
2 tablespoons cornstarch
3 large eggs plus 1 large egg yolk, at room temperature
¼ teaspoon vanilla extract
Softened butter, for the foil
¼ cup apricot preserves

1. Wrap the bottom of a 7-inch springform pan tightly with heavy-duty aluminum foil. Butter the inside of the pan with all of the melted butter. Sprinkle the bottom of the pan with the cookie crumbs.

2. In a 5- to 7-quart pressure cooker, combine the apricots and water. Bring to high pressure over high heat. Adjust the heat to maintain the pressure. Cook for 30 seconds. Remove from the heat and quick-release the pressure. Open the lid, tilting it away from you to block any escaping steam. Drain the mixture in a wire sieve set over a medium bowl; reserve the liquid. Transfer 3 tablespoons of the apricots to a food processor fitted with the metal blade. Set the remaining apricots aside.

3. Add the cream cheese and sugar to the food processor. Process until smooth, stopping the machine occasionally to scrape down the sides of the bowl. Add the sour cream and cornstarch and pulse until combined. With the machine running, add the eggs, one at a time, then the yolk and vanilla, scraping down the bowl as needed. Spread evenly in the prepared pan.

4. Butter a 15-inch-long piece of aluminum foil. Tightly cover the pan with the foil, buttered side down, allowing some room for expansion at the top for the cheesecake to rise. (The foil should completely cover the pan.)

5. Place the trivet in the bottom of the pot. Pour 2 cups of water into the pot. Center the covered dish in an aluminum foil "cradle" (see page 113). Using the cradle, lower the pan onto the trivet.

6. Lock the lid in place. Bring to high pressure over high heat. Adjust the heat to maintain the pressure. Cook for 25 minutes. Remove from the heat. Allow the pressure to drop naturally, about 20 minutes. Open the lid, tilting it away from you to block any escaping steam.

7. Using the cradle, lift the pan out of the pot. Let stand for 2 or 3 minutes. Remove the foil. If necessary, blot any water on the surface of the cheesecake with a paper towel. Run a sharp knife around the inside of the pan to release the cheesecake from the

sides. Place on a wire cake rack and cool completely.

8. Remove the sides of the pan. Cover the cheesecake with plastic wrap and refrigerate until well chilled, at least 4 hours.

9. To make the glaze, in a medium saucepan, combine the apricot preserves, reserved apricots, and 3 tablespoons of the apricot cooking liquid. Bring to a boil over medium heat and stir until slightly thickened, about 1 minute. Place the cheesecake on a serving plate. Spread the apricot glaze over the top of the cheesecake, letting a little of the glaze drip down the sides. Let stand at room temperature for about 30 minutes. Serve, using a sharp knife dipped into hot water to cut each slice.

——

Makes 6 to 8 servings
25 minutes at high pressure

café con leche flan

I f you need convincing that pressure cookers do an incredible job of preparing silky-smooth custards, make these coffee-flavored flans—the proof is in the pudding.

Butter, for the ramekins
½ cup plus ⅓ cup sugar
2 tablespoons cold water
1½ teaspoons instant espresso powder (see Note)
2 teaspoons boiling water
2 large eggs, at room temperature
1 cup half-and-half, heated until simmering
½ teaspoon vanilla
Pinch of ground cinnamon (optional)

1. Lightly butter four ½-cup ramekins or custard cups and set aside.

2. Place ½ cup sugar in a medium saucepan and sprinkle with the 2 tablespoons cold water. Cook over medium-high heat, stirring constantly, just until the mixture is boiling. Cook without stirring, occasionally swirling the saucepan by the handle to combine the darker syrup at the edges with the clear syrup in the center, until the caramel is evenly golden brown, about 3 minutes. Immediately pour equal amounts of the hot caramel into the prepared cups. Quickly tilt each cup to partially coat the inside with caramel.

3. In a small bowl, dissolve the espresso powder in the boiling water. In a medium bowl, whisk the eggs and the remaining ⅓ cup sugar. Gradually whisk in the hot half-and-half, then the dissolved espresso, vanilla, and cinnamon, if desired. Strain the custard mixture through a fine wire sieve into a large glass measuring cup to remove any bits of egg white, and divide evenly among the cups. Cover each cup tightly with aluminum foil.

4. Place the trivet and steamer basket in a 5- to 7-quart pressure cooker. Pour 2 cups water into the cooker. Stack the cups, pyramid-style, in the cooker. Lock the lid in place. Bring to high pressure over high heat. Adjust the heat to maintain the pressure. Cook for 8 minutes. Remove from the heat and quick-release the pressure. Open the lid, tilting it away from you to block any escaping steam. Let the flans stand in the cooker for about 3 minutes to cool.

5. Using kitchen tongs, remove the cups from the cooker. Remove the foil. The centers of the flans should be very slightly underdone and wobble when shaken. If necessary, re-cover with foil, return to the cooker, and cook at high pressure for an additional 1 minute. If there is a small puddle of water on the surface of a flan, carefully blot it with a paper towel.

6. Cool the flans to room temperature. Cover each with plastic wrap and refrigerate until chilled, at least 4 hours.

7. To serve, run a sharp, thin knife around the inside of each cup to release the flan. One at a time, invert the flans onto a serving plate. Hold the cup onto the plate and give a sharp shake to unmold the flan and its caramel syrup.

Note: Instant espresso powder is available at Italian grocers and specialty food stores. If unavailable, substitute 2 teaspoons regular instant coffee.

Makes 4 servings
8 minutes at high pressure

caramel knowledge

Making the caramel for the self-contained sauce in a flan or crème caramel is very simple, but here are some tips to side-step any mistakes.

➤ Have the custard cups buttered and ready, and pour in the hot caramel without delay, as it will thicken quickly as it cools.

➤ Don't stir the sugar syrup after it comes to a boil—that encourages crystallization. If you want to mix the syrup, swirl the pot by its handle.

➤ With this caramel, you can ignore any crystals that form inside the pan. If you prefer, you may use a pastry brush dipped in hot water, pressing hard against the side of the pan, to wash them down into the boiling syrup.

➤ To check the caramel for doneness, you do not need a candy thermometer—use your eyes and nose. The darker the caramel, the deeper the flavor. It should look golden brown and have a distinct, sharp aroma that seems on the verge of burning.

ginger crème brûlée

When the culinary history of the late twentieth century is written, surely crème brûlée will emerge as one of our era's favorites. This version gets an added fillip from crystallized ginger, available at Asian markets, specialty stores, and many supermarkets. Two tips: The brown sugar topping will melt more evenly if the sugar is allowed to stand uncovered at room temperature for a few hours or overnight to dry it out. And placing the ramekins in a pan of ice cubes keeps the custard chilled while the sugar melts in the broiler.

1½ cups heavy cream
4 large egg yolks
¼ cup granulated sugar
½ teaspoon vanilla extract
3 tablespoons finely chopped crystallized ginger
3 tablespoons packed light brown sugar

1. In a small saucepan over medium heat, bring the cream to a simmer. In a medium bowl, whisk the yolks, sugar, and vanilla to combine. Gradually whisk in the hot cream. Strain through a wire sieve into a large glass measuring cup, and pour evenly into four ½-cup ramekins or custard cups. Divide the ginger evenly among the ramekins. Cover each ramekin tightly with aluminum foil.

2. Place the trivet and steamer basket in a 5- to 7-quart pressure cooker. Pour 2 cups water into the cooker. Stack the cups, pyramid-style, in the cooker. Lock the lid in place. Bring to high pressure over high heat. Adjust the heat to maintain the pressure. Cook for 8 minutes. Remove from the heat and quick-release the pressure. Open the lid, tilting it away from you to block any escaping steam. Let the custards stand in the pot for 3 minutes for easier handling. Using kitchen tongs, remove the cups from the cooker. Remove the foil. The centers should wobble slightly—they will set as they cool. If necessary, recover with foil, return to the cooker, and cook for an additional 1 minute at high pressure. Cool the custards to room temperature. Cover each with plastic wrap and refrigerate until chilled, at least 4 hours.

3. When ready to serve, position a broiler rack about 6 inches from the source of heat and preheat the broiler. Unwrap the custards. Rub the brown sugar through a small wire sieve, coating the top of each custard with a layer of sugar. Place the ramekins in a baking pan, and surround them with ice cubes.

4. Broil the custards, watching carefully to avoid scorching, until the sugar melts, 1 to 2 minutes. Remove the ramekins from the baking pan and serve immediately.

Makes 4 servings
8 minutes at high pressure

creamy **rice pudding**

n Europe, many cooks simmer their rice pudding on the stove, making a firm pudding that doesn't need any eggs to add richness. This pressure-cooked version of the method is best cooked on low pressure to avoid scorching the milk and sugar, but see the Note following the recipe if your cooker has only one setting. Use a medium-grain rice that has plenty of starch. Possibilities include Latino brands (such as Goya) or imported Italian or Spanish varieties (Arborio, Baldo, Carnaroli, Vialone Nano, Valencia, or "paella" rice). Personalize the pudding to suit your taste. Leave out the cinnamon, or substitute dried cranberries or cherries for the raisins and orange for the lemon zest.

> 4 cups milk, plus more as needed
> 1½ cups medium-grain rice (do not rinse)
> 1 cup sugar
> Grated zest of 1 lemon
> ½ teaspoon salt
> ½ cup raisins or golden raisins
> 2 teaspoons vanilla extract
> ¼ teaspoon ground cinnamon
> Approximately 1½ cups heavy cream, half-and-half, or milk, for serving

1. In a 5- to 7-quart pressure cooker, mix the 4 cups milk with the rice, sugar, lemon zest, and salt.

2. Lock the lid in place. Bring to low pressure over high heat. (See Note.) Adjust the heat to maintain the pressure. Cook for 11 minutes. Remove from the heat. Quick-release the pressure. Open the lid, tilting it away from you to block any escaping steam. If the rice isn't tender, replace the lid (no need to lock it) and let stand for 10 to 15 minutes, allowing the residual heat to continue cooking the rice. Do not return to the heat. Add the raisins, vanilla, and cinnamon and stir well. If serving warm, transfer to a serving dish. If desired, cool the pudding, cover, and refrigerate until chilled, at least 2 hours. Whether warm or chilled, if the pudding seems too firm, stir in enough additional milk to reach the desired consistency.

3. Serve the pudding in bowls, topping each serving with a few tablespoons of cream or milk.

Note: If you have only a high-pressure setting on your cooker, butter the inside of the cooker. Cook the rice mixture for 4 minutes on high pressure. Remove from the heat. Let the pressure release naturally.

Makes 6 to 8 servings
11 minutes at low pressure

"no-cook" orchard applesauce

Applesauce is a comforting snack. We call this "no cook" because all you do is bring the apples to high pressure in the cooker, then turn it off immediately. You can use any apple you like (just not Red Delicious, which are best for eating and make a mealy sauce), but the recipe is probably best with a combination. For example, sweet Golden Delicious apples match well with tart Pippins or Empires. Or try juicy Jonathan apples with sweet MacIntosh. The final flavor varies according to the apples used, so be flexible—you may have to simmer the sauce a few minutes to reduce excess liquid and intensify the apple flavor (there goes the "no cook" theory!).

> **6 medium (2½ pounds total) apples, peeled, cored, and cut into ¼-inch-thick wedges**
> **½ cup water**
> **½ cup sugar**
> **1 cinnamon stick or ⅛ teaspoon ground cinnamon**
> **One 4-inch strip lemon zest, removed from the lemon with a vegetable peeler**

1. In a 5- to 7-quart pressure cooker, combine the apples, water, sugar, cinnamon stick, and lemon zest. Lock the lid in place. Bring to high pressure over high heat. Immediately remove from the heat and quick-release the pressure. Open the lid, tilting it away from you to block any escaping steam. Discard the cinnamon stick and lemon zest. Stir well to break up the apples. If desired, return the pot, uncovered, to high heat and bring to a boil. Cook, stirring often, until the applesauce has thickened to the desired consistency. Serve warm. Or cool to room temperature, cover, and refrigerate until chilled, about 2 hours.

_____

Makes about 2½ cups
Bring to high pressure, then quick-release

riesling pears with mascarpone and almonds

I f you are looking for a delicious, easy dessert with only a few well-chosen ingredients, this is it. Add speedy preparation to these qualities, and the result is a dessert you'll return to again and again, especially for dinner parties where you need to present something elegant with a minimum of fuss. The better the wine, the better the results. Use 1 cup to cook the pears, then chill and serve the remainder in small glasses with the dessert.

> ⅓ cup sliced almonds
> 4 medium firm-ripe Bosc pears
> 1 lemon, cut in half
> 1 cup fruity semi-dry white wine, such as
>   Johannesburg Riesling
> ¼ cup sugar
> 6 ounces mascarpone cheese, at room temperature
> Mint sprigs, for garnish

1. Position a rack in the center of the oven and preheat to 350°F. Spread the almonds on a baking sheet. Bake, stirring occasionally, until the almonds are toasted, about 10 minutes. Transfer the almonds to a plate and cool completely. Set aside.

2. Peel the pears and cut in half lengthwise. Using a melon baller, remove the tough core from each pear half. Rub the pears with the lemon halves to prevent discoloring.

3. In a 5- to 7-quart pressure cooker, combine the wine and sugar. Arrange the pears in the cooker and spoon the wine over them. Lock the lid in place. Bring to high pressure over high heat. Adjust the heat to maintain the pressure. Cook for 1 minute. Remove from the heat and quick-release the pressure.

Open the lid, tilting it away from you to block any escaping steam. Using a slotted spoon, transfer to a deep platter. Pour the wine syrup over the pears and cool completely. Cover with plastic wrap and refrigerate until chilled, at least 1 hour or overnight.

4. To serve, place two pear halves, cut sides up, in a shallow bowl. Fill the hollow of each pear with a dollop of mascarpone and sprinkle with almonds. Drizzle with some of the wine syrup and garnish with the mint. Repeat with the remaining ingredients. Serve chilled.

———————

Makes 4 servings
1 minute at high pressure

index

index

table of equivalents

The exact equivalents in the following tables have been rounded for convenience.

LIQUID/DRY MEASURES

U.S.	METRIC
¼ teaspoon	1.25 milliliters
½ teaspoon	2.5 milliliters
1 teaspoon	5 milliliters
1 tablespoon (3 teaspoons)	15 milliliters
1 fluid ounce (2 tablespoons)	30 milliliters
¼ cup	60 milliliters
⅓ cup	80 milliliters
½ cup	120 milliliters
1 cup	240 milliliters
1 pint (2 cups)	480 milliliters
1 quart (4 cups, 32 ounces)	960 milliliters
1 gallon (4 quarts)	3.84 liters
1 ounce (by weight)	28 grams
1 pound	454 grams
2.2 pounds	1 kilogram

OVEN TEMPERATURE

FAHRENHEIT	CELSIUS	GAS
250	120	½
275	140	1
300	150	2
325	160	3
350	180	4
375	190	5
400	200	6
425	220	7
450	230	8
475	240	9
500	260	10

LENGTH

U.S.	METRIC
⅛ inch	3 millimeters
¼ inch	6 millimeters
½ inch	12 millimeters
1 inch	2.5 centimeters